BEHIND
BLUE EYES

BEHIND BLUE EYES

MARK S. MILLER

The Sheathed Quill Press

Houston, Texas

ISBN (Paperback Edition) 978-0-9992445-0-0

Editing by Sean Guillemette, Connie Kaloudis and Quang Vo
Cover image by Sofia Fanzo
All photographs by Mark S. Miller
Book design by Sean Guillemette

Printed and bound in the USA
Published 2017

Published by The Sheathed Quill Press
P.O. Box 5298
Kingwood, Texas 77325
USA
Email: info@thesheathedquill.com

Visit www.thesheathedquill.com

Whether I shall turn out to be the hero of my own life, or whether that station will be held by anybody else, these pages must show.

—Charles Dickens, *David Copperfield*

CONTENTS

PART III   BEHIND BLUE EYES

ACKNOWLEDGEMENTS

Throughout my journey, I was grateful to the many friends and colleagues who encouraged me to stay the course and to let my adventurous soul shine. But, above all, I would like to thank my wonderful children Stephen, Chelsea and Kevin, as well as my grandchildren Patrick and Henry, for always making me smile and especially for their patience and understanding my need for adventure. I hope one day you will read my book and take a page and fly with it.

I want to also thank my mom, Cornelia Miller, for her unconditional love, continued support, and most importantly, her insistence that I follow my ambitions and dreams during the course of my childhood, and who still to this day continues to support my decisions. Knowing I have her support matters most to me.

I would like to thank my family, especially my Aunt Patricia, who now lives in Heaven, and my Aunt Mary Ann, for not only their support but also their encouraging words throughout my Adventure. A smile instantly came to my face the moment I received an email from either one of them.

I would like to acknowledge and give special thanks to Connie Kaloudis and Sean Guillemette for their thoughts, comments and most of all their patience in making this book happen. I also owe a huge thank you to Sofia Fanzo who is responsible for the cover of this book and to The Sheathed Quill Press for publishing it. It would not have been possible without all of you.

INTRODUCTION

There is a time in every person's life when one needs to step back and take a survey of oneself—to unplug from one's daily existence. Hopefully, this won't drive you towards the severities of a monastic life but rather a course correction of your life journey. It has for me.

What follows is a journey that began as a manuscript—Jerry McGuire style—with many co-workers thinking I had totally gone mad.

My Jerry McGuire manuscript led me to travel on a working container ship as a way to get to Europe, then traveling the back roads of South Africa, Mozambique, Uganda and Tanzania for nearly five months in order to take a break from over 25 years of being a lawyer. This is more than a travel diary of my crazy Adventure. It is a book for individuals in demanding positions, specifically for lawyers, illustrating the importance of taking a break from the day-to-day grind of billing hours to appreciate life from a new and refreshed perspective.

My Adventure was not about any mystical insight into life, nor a religious transformation. We could debate whether this was a mental breakdown (but seriously it wasn't). My Adventure was simply an adult time-out.

Faith is taking the first step even when you don't see the whole staircase.
—Martin Luther King, Jr.

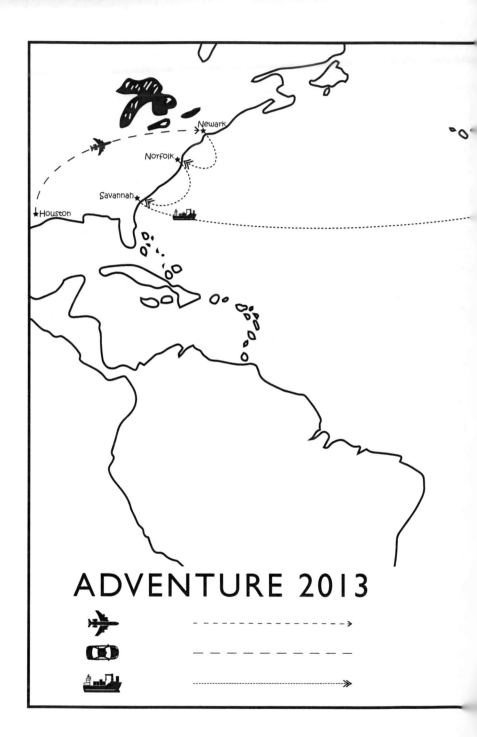

ADVENTURE 2013

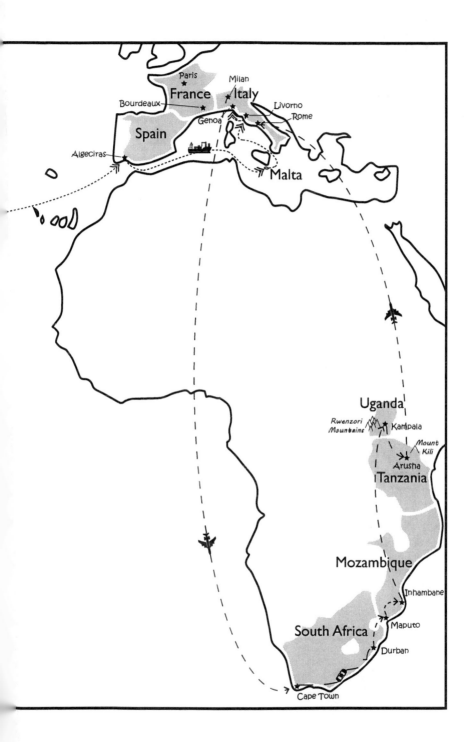

PROLOGUE

I awoke clinging to the side of my bed. Every item not bolted was being slammed against the dark grey walls of my room. My iPad flew off the end table missing my face by inches, landing on a pile of clean clothes that left my closet and were now scattered across the floor. As my white knuckles gripped the side of my dorm-like bed waiting for death to find me, I questioned, *Why had I taken this Adventure? Had I completely messed up a great legal career all for the sake of taking time away from work? Why did I think travel via a container ship from North America to Europe with 20 crew members who spoke very little English and a retired high school teacher would be a good idea?*

With commanding intensity, the angry waves continuously smashed against the side of the container ship, their power growing with every crash. I was convinced that most of the 4,000 containers on this 250-meter long ship were now floating in the middle of the Atlantic Ocean. Hurricane Ike in 2008 was no match. I couldn't help but think *I totally f***ed up my entire life.*

I closed my eyes and prayed for the storm to pass.

As the waves crashed against my cabin and water seeped through my windows, a brief moment of sanity overcame me. In that moment, I realized that the intensity of a storm in life is strongest immediately before the calm. In one's legal career, one should never quit simply because billing hours reaches that epic point where one can no longer tolerate ONE MORE TIME ENTRY. Instead, one should take an adult time-out and experience how a fierce storm can move one into

a unique calmness and joy. This is how I handled my career storm
in early 2013.

*A lot of us first aspired to far-ranging travel and exotic adventure early
in our teens...Thus, when we allow ourselves to imagine as we once did,
we know, with a sudden jarring clarity, that if we don't go right now, we're
never going to do it. And we'll be haunted by our unrealized dreams...*

—Tim Cahill

Calm seas in the Atlantic.

PART I

THE MANUSCRIPT

CHAPTER ONE

BACKGROUND

In March of 2013, I turned 52, and some could say I was in the middle of a mid-life crisis. Maybe or maybe not, but it really didn't matter to me. I could have spent hours with a therapist exploring my issues and eventually come to some "rational" explanation of what the f*** I was doing and why. Instead, I decided to pursue a different route.

Remember: It's Your Ride

I grew up in a Seattle suburb, attended Washington State University, immediately proceeded to law school and then to NYU for a tax degree. Following NYU, I began my legal career at a law firm where I am a tax partner (the "Firm"). I performed life as expected. I played sports in high school, did well at each level of school, advanced to the next level of education and obtained a job at one of the nation's most prestigious law firms specializing in ERISA law.[1] I was the picture of an ideal person, a dedicated and committed lawyer

---

1 ERISA is a federal law that governs certain employee benefit plans and programs. It is a specialized and complex type of practice that involves an office, a desk and a headset that is used for the 2,000-plus hours billed on a yearly basis.

at a great Firm who loved his career and a loyal family man with three beautiful kids. I took pride in that I was determined to have one house and one job. It was my recipe for a happy, simple and successful life.

The Practice of Big Law

Being an ERISA lawyer is very rewarding, and I found much enjoyment in this area of law. I felt fortunate to work at an international law firm that as of April of 2017, has close to 4,000 lawyers worldwide. Firms similar to mine are commonly referred to as "Big Law." My practice was cutting edge in many ways. My clients were sophisticated, posed interesting issues, and I felt privileged to work with them. Having great relationships with clients made practicing law fun and exciting. I credit part of my success with clients to what I learned from a book I read on client development. The book encouraged lawyers to become *trusted advisors* in contrast to being a hired gun. A hired gun was a lawyer hired for a single shot, be it the company litigation case or a complex corporate transaction. The author advocated that when a lawyer takes on the role as trusted advisor, the client would direct all legal work faced by the client to other lawyers within the same firm and thus would generate additional billable hours for the firm. This made perfect sense to me.

Come Back New

I became that trusted advisor, and it worked magnificently. I was dealing with client issues and relationships between the client and other internal Firm lawyers, and billings increased dramatically. From an economic viewpoint, all was good.

However, the trusted advisor role was killing me. I began taking on all the concerns and problem-solving matters for clients. Many clients mentioned—on way too many occasions—"Just call Mark. He'll take care of it." As for billable hours, this was great but dealing with these collateral issues became overwhelming. I went from being a lawyer to becoming a personal counselor. The process evolved until I was more concerned about the issue than the client was. I had taken the trusted advisor role too far. Someone once told me when you become more concerned with solving an issue than the person with the actual issue, you need to back away and let them take the responsibility in resolving their own issue. Don't get me wrong—I didn't stop caring or stop doing quality legal work, I just needed a break from the evolution of my trusted advisor role. I had become trapped, and I did not see a way out. My sense of loyalty and commitment in being a team player paralyzed me. My work had evolved into a job as opposed to a legal career, and I have always believed that once a lawyer viewed his/her employment as a job instead of a legal career, it was time to move on. I needed to catch my breath. I needed change and I needed it ASAP.

In the six months leading to my request for a Gap Period, I had many loud wake-up calls that things were off with work. I am a strong believer that the universe gives hints on what you need to do or change, and when you ignore the signs, the messages get louder and stronger until one day a two-by-four smacks you in the forehead with the message you've been ignoring. I had one of these two-by-four moments.

In early January of 2013, on a cold and rainy Friday afternoon, after a long day of work in my Firm's London office, I decided to catch a play in the West End, *War Horse,* before packing for my flight back to Houston in the morning. The play was spectacular and had me so pumped that I stopped at a pub and had a pint. When I arrived back to the flat, I checked my Outlook for messages, and I had received an email from a newly hired general counsel of one of my long-standing clients. His email berated me on how my Firm's invoices were formatted (which had been done in the same fashion for the last 25 years) and "reminded" me that he was the chief legal counsel for the company and had all the obligations and responsibilities that go along with this position.

In all my years as a lawyer I had never received an email like this. I immediately called my day-to-day contact person who was copied on the email. He apologized upon answering my call and suggested that I contact the general counsel, wondering that maybe he was having a bad day. I made the call only to find out it wasn't a mistake. I couldn't help but think that I can take on their ERISA issues, get them out of all kinds of f***ups and then receive an email like this—all about the format of my Firm's invoices? At that moment, I knew I needed a break. This trusted advisor role was just burning me out.

Around the same time, several local law firms became interested in hiring me. I had spent over 25 years at the same job, basically in the same office, and felt that maybe a new environment would reinvigorate me. So I decided to test the market.

I was wined and dined and offered salaries that were intoxicating. Though, I was really second fiddle to their ultimate desire—more clients. They only wanted to exploit my book of business. The entire process became more stress than I could manage. After several interviews, large dinners and drinks, I concluded that changing law firms was not the solution to my frustration. What I really needed was a break from law. I was determined not to wake up at age 65 wondering where my life went.

In January of 2013, I was driving home from a friend's house late one night and The Who song "Behind Blue Eyes" was playing on the radio, and it made my heart skip. Listening to that song was the exact moment (and I mean the exact moment) I realized I was going to take a modern day adult time-out and rediscover the man behind *my* blue eyes.

People who travel the world aren't running away from life. Just the opposite. Those that break the mold, explore the world, and live on their own terms are running toward true living, in my opinion. We have a degree of freedom a lot of people will never experience. We get to be the captains of our ships. But it is a freedom we chose to have. We looked around and said, "I want something different." It was that freedom and attitude I saw in travelers years ago that inspired me to do what I am doing now. I saw them break the mold and I thought to myself, "Why not me too?" I'm not running away. I am running towards the world and my idea of life.
                                                            —Nomadic Matt, Blogger

So what is this book all about? What I am writing about consists of three parts. Part I are the steps that I took to take a break from my career. Part II is about the most memorable parts of my adult time-out, and Part III is about the person that I discovered behind these blue eyes. Overall, this is a story of me becoming a Modern Day Adventurer. A story of how I transcended from being a simple billing machine to choosing freedom and exploration as a way of being in this world while maintaining an increasingly complex, sophisticated and satisfying law practice.

The tragedy of life doesn't lie in not reaching your goal. The tragedy lies in having no goal to reach.

—Benjamin E. Mays

CHAPTER TWO

———————

THE STEPS

A partner in his or her 50s is generally in the sweet spot as a profitable billing machine. Throughout the years, my Firm and its clients could count on me to provide exceptional service without complaint or hesitation, no matter what time of day it was, or how long it took to complete the task at hand, thus producing an incredible amount of hours billed. However, this pace of life drove me to wanting a complete and utter disengagement from Big Law, and not just a two-week vacation, but an exemplified absence. Most lawyers simply quit as a mechanism to cope with the pressures and frustrations of Big Law. Despite the tempting offers I received from competing law firms, it was clear to me that I did not want to quit, and I felt that I had already chosen the right Firm to spend my career and had no intention or desire of abandoning my Firm. But I needed to do something to regain my drive. I concluded that I needed time away from the office, from the pressures of Big Law, from my exhausted mind, and so I requested an adult time-out, which to my knowledge, had never been granted nor considered at my Firm in the past. My request was definitely extreme and drastic (or some would say desperate) and came from deep out in left field. It was a huge leap of faith hoping that nothing bad would happen professionally or personally in (a) asking for and (b) taking a time-out.

I, however, needed to figure out how to formally make my request. While exploring the best methods to approach this unprecedented request, I was amazed at the lack of resources (almost all the resources were on how to transition from one law firm to another or to an in-house legal position but not on requesting a leave). So, I decided to come up with my own steps which I used as a framework for my request (these steps became the basis for my manuscript described below). The 13 steps are as follows:

1. It Is None of My Business What You Think of Me

It took me a while to grasp this concept, but it was a key and central concept. People were more than willing to share their thoughts on how *I* was to live my life, what *I* should say and what *I* should do. Some lectured on how crazy I was to take an adult time-out in the prime of my legal career—and they may have been right—but as long as I was thinking about what others thought of me and what I thought they were *expecting* of me, the further I strayed from my inner self.

As I developed my plan, I became judicious in telling people what I was up to. I became less tolerant of their comments, thoughts and/or suggestions even when I had their full support. I learned to embrace this step based on the principle that it was none of *my* business what anyone thought about my Adventure. Plain and simple. I was (am) determined to live by this step and not question what others thought of my Adventure. Once this step is mastered, you will experience an unprecedented freedom and will live the life you are meant to live.

2. Hesitation Gets You Nowhere

Once it was clear I was going to take a break, I immediately acted. Allowing something this big to drag in conversation would have killed the spirit of my Adventure. I did not hesitate. I did not second guess myself. I knew what I wanted, and more importantly, what I needed.

I was determined to take this Gap Year regardless of pay and benefits or even if I would be required to leave work altogether (I am, however, very grateful that the leaving part never came to pass). When I first spoke to the managing partner about my Gap Year, he asked for a memo (which I reference as my manuscript). I delivered it promptly and followed up with him immediately regarding his decision. I explained how I wanted to give each client a three-month notice of my leave, and I wanted my leave to begin in mid-April. Providing a clear timeline and standing firm on my request blocked the opportunity to drag the decision-making process on ad infinitum. Not only is it good to have a quick resolution in mind, but it is also equally or more important to get the decision promptly as well.

When I think of the leaders and mentors in my life, one common trait is that they do not hesitate with decision-making. That is what I did. The entire process from the idea, to the conversation, to the approval was less than five business days. Hesitation in Big Law is a death by a thousand cuts, and you will not end up being or doing what you truly want should you hesitate.

3. Replace Fear with Curiosity

This step reminds me of a book I read 15 or so years ago titled *Feel the Fear and Do It Anyway* by Susan Jeffers, Ph.D. I don't really remember the substance of the book, but I never forgot the title—the title says it all. There were times I thought during this "ask" phase, *What the hell am I doing?* Thoughts of messing up a great legal career with appreciable pay by asking for and then proceeding with a Gap Period raced through my mind. Once I realized these were merely fear thoughts, I replaced them with thoughts of curiosity.

As I took on curiosity as a way of being (and thinking) in this ask phase, the request for a Gap Year (and then actually taking the Gap Period) became less fearful and more interesting. I became curious as to how this whole Gap Year would turn out—what it would be like to walk into the unknown for a year and then back into Big Law. I began to replace thoughts of fear with *let's see what happens*.

Buzz Aldrin, an astronaut who did the moon walk back in 1969, recently spoke at my youngest son's college graduation. He asked the graduates to think of their future as full of unknown possibilities along with a sense of curiosity, just like how NASA looked at going to the moon when no one had quite done so in the past. He spoke of imagining what comes after the letter "Z" in the alphabet like going to where no one had gone before and, more importantly, where no one imagined one could go.

Pushing past fears and becoming curious as to what comes next and taking steps towards the unknown is an adventurous way to live and the way life ought to be lived. It is about boundary pushing and not being content with the confines of the ordinary.

We all have a choice whether to be curious or fearful about an outcome that we have no control over. I chose to be curious and pushed the boundaries of the ordinary when I made my request. (I have always been a glass half-full type of person. In fact, I am a person who believes that my cup runneth over. I also thought after taking this Adventure, I would become the Firm's spokesperson for its "Work/ Life Balance Program"—now that would be funny).

4. The Pope Benedict Rule (or Exception)

During my decision-making process, Pope Benedict announced to the world that he was stepping down as pope and gave *only* three weeks' notice. It had been customary that every pope die in office, and that is what every pope had done for the past 600 years (I guess it is part of the job description), but not Pope Benedict. He was leaving the papacy on two feet instead of ten toes up (I'm sure Vatican HR were confused with this new protocol). Now if anyone questions the shortness of your notice period, note to your supervisor that the pope only gave three weeks' notice of his resignation, and *he* was the leader of the entire Catholic Church. But the notice period is not the focus of this step. This step is about choosing a path forward on your own terms.

I decided during this "ask" phase that I needed to embrace a little Pope Benedict and not follow the expected path of exiting the Firm according to the normal flow: being asked to leave (i.e. being fired), death (although Firm partner funerals are an amazing event; it is almost worth dying for), withdrawing to move to a competing law firm (i.e. getting pissed off at the Firm, quitting and taking clients to spite the Firm) or simply retiring. When I read what the pope was doing, it was the confirmation that I too could be bold and go where no partner had gone before—a working leave of absence.

When the managing partner asked me what precedent there was for this leave, all I could think of were maternity leaves or the occasional rehab stint. Since those leaves didn't apply to me, I became Pope Benedict-like and broke new ground on partner behavior by asking for and then taking an adult time-out. Whether this step is a rule or an exception, living life based on actions that test (challenge) historical (and unspoken) precedent is much more fun than going along with the same old, same old of how prior generations have lived Big Law.

5. Past Performance Is a Predictor of Future Actions (Notwithstanding What Investment People Tell You)

As an ERISA lawyer, I participate in many investment committees for pension and 401(k) plans. Typically, an investment professional meets quarterly with a plan's investment committee to review the last quarter's investment returns. At the bottom of each page of the investment report is a statement that says something to the effect that "Past performance is not an indication of future investment results." In other words, just because ABC Fund returned 20 percent last quarter, there is no guarantee that the fund will duplicate that same return in the future. We all know this. But *in reality,* each investment committee bases its decision to keep a particular investment on the fund's historic investment track record. Investment committees rarely change an investment lineup as there is no getting away from making decisions based on past performances.

Think of your own personal 401(k)/IRA or another investment account. When was the last time you reallocated your investments into a different investment or a completely new investment strategy? Inertia takes control and change just does not happen.

The point is that one's past performance in life will forecast one's future *unless* one consciously changes and creates a future not tied to what one has or has not done in the past. You *can* create something completely new and exciting unconnected to the past. We can all choose a future based on possibilities and not past performance. If not, your next ten years at work will mimic the past ten years.

In the months leading up to my decision, it became abundantly clear that the next ten years of being a lawyer was going to look similar to my past ten. Sure, a few parts would change slightly, and some lawyers would be hired, fired and retired, but nothing was really going to change—unless I made change happen. Taking this Gap Period was a great first step in shaking things up and doing things differently. I was committed to no longer just hanging on until retirement or replaying life as an ERISA lawyer because I knew what that life looked like. I was about *not* repeating the past but living a different future. Living a life full of possibilities.

Some say Albert Einstein defined insanity as doing the same thing over and over and hoping for a different outcome. I was committed to stopping my insanity by not doing or being the way I was and hoping for a different outcome. I did not want my past performance to dictate my future decisions, dreams and ambitions.

6. Be Happy Rather Than Right

I struggled with "doing the right thing" in the Firm's eyes by just toughing it out until I had enough and either quitting or being asked to leave. Too many people, myself included, seem to choose being right over being happy. And in January of 2013, I was all about reversing course and choosing happiness over being right. Being right (at all costs) seldom leads to happiness. And what lawyers do in the vein of being right in life is to blow up a career at their firm by quitting in frustration. I did not want to take this route. I wanted instead to wake up excited and driven to tackle new projects and create new opportunities for my law practice. But in January of 2013, my energy tank was empty and a Gap Period was the first step in refueling it on the road to happiness.

Deep inside me there was an adventurous soul, and I realized that my true essence had been covered up with 25-plus years as a billing machine. It was time to choose happiness over the Firm's expectations of partners—the world of bill, bill and bill some more.

Ultimately, I felt I needed to take a Gap Period in order to restore my happiness. Was it wrong to take a Gap Period at my age? Was it wrong to leave clients and the Firm? I could have been right to think so. But in choosing happiness over doing the right thing, I was able to regain the edge of serving clients at a level unparalleled to my peers while at the same time becoming a modern day adventurer.

7. Start Having the Time of Your Life

I have been told by many lawyers that they love their job too much to take a break or they would never be able to take a break because of work obligations, and while that may be true on a micro basis, I strongly disagree when looking at the big picture of taking a break from a 35-year legal career. Taking my Gap Year was not about destroying a great legal career or burning bridges with colleagues and clients that have been good to me. It was about living my life to my fullest potential and expanding my walls.

This step seems fairly straightforward. However, in reality, I was putting off living and having fun until that magical retirement age of 65. In making my Gap Period happen, I shifted my focus from simply sustaining an existence to creating a life full of adventure, fun and excitement. I gave up the grinning and bearing of work until my pension kicked in. I proved to myself that it was possible to have the time of my life and not have to quit work to achieve it. Taking a time-out allowed me to see this reality. My Gap Period accelerated fun in my life and left me wanting more in all aspects of my life.

8. Become the Most Interesting Person in the World

After 25-plus years of being a dynamic ERISA lawyer (one should laugh at this), I evolved into a working and billing machine. In other words, I became quite good at the lawyer gig, but outside of law, I was not an interesting person. A close friend of mine commented that she expected my Gap Period would make me the most interesting person in the world. Those words hit deep within my soul. There was a time back in college and law school when I was really fun and interesting to be around, and I had done some real adventurous traveling. Somehow a slow and uninteresting death fell upon my soul with each billable hour. In January of 2013, I decided to change things and reawaken my soul and make my Gap Period a modern day adventure. I was going to become a true adventurer and travel to places I had never heard of and become interesting once again—not for anyone else other than myself (all the while keeping things moving at work, of course).

9. It's Your Future, Go Get It—and Prepare to Smile

This was my future, my life, and I was going to reach out and grab it. I was not going to *do* my career as a loyal Firm citizen abiding by the unspoken and unwritten rules of sucking up all frustrations of Big Law before being driven from the Firm by (a) quitting to join a competitor, (b) being forced out, (c) dying or (d) retiring with a nice pension. I saw too many lawyers *doing* and *being* according to this unwritten code of Firm conduct, and I was one of those lawyers. But by actually taking my future into my own hands and consciously thinking about what I wanted, I began to live. Living by my rules and grasping for the things that were important to me was liberating. My eyes became wide open for the first time in many years. A colleague of mine commented that I "must have an extra chromosome" in my brain to actually ask for and ultimately create my Gap Period. I'm not sure about an extra chromosome, but it definitely took some moxie.

10. Slow Is Smooth and Smooth Is Fast

I was making a climb on what is known as Namche Hill, which was the first of many multiple hour treks up mountains in the Khumbu Valley on the way to Everest Base Camp. Namche Hill was an extremely difficult climb. Our guide lectured to my group of six that we were moving too fast, and we needed to slow our pace down. He began to use the phrase "slow is smooth and smooth is fast" over and over until us green trekkers figured it out—and it worked. Since then, I have applied this phrase to many areas of my life. When I decided to ask for my Gap Year, I took the planning process slowly and thoughtfully. A smooth plan evolved and before I knew it my adult time-out was approved (but we'll speak more on that later). Friends remarked at how quickly I pulled this off, but in reality, the process was *slow and smooth* and then it happened—*smooth is fast*. If I were to ever get a tattoo, this would be it.

11. Rethink Possible

I have turned my BlackBerry off and on a thousand times and the phrase "Rethink Possible" always lights up on the screen. In developing my Gap Year, I took this marketing slogan to heart. Rethink Possible is asking one to think of *possibility* in a different manner. This is a crucial step. A lot of things are possible in one's life and so *is taking a Gap Year*. One could weigh less, run faster, move to a different law firm and the list could go on and on. But only when I began to rethink what was possible, did I get the notion, nerve, guts, etc. to truly consider what I could create in terms of a leave from the daily grind of billing hours.

I rethought what was possible and how to *actually* make it happen. It is similar to the saying "you can only go as far as your imagination will let you." Dropping the limiting thoughts of what others would think/ say and why it would not be approved and replacing it with positive self-talk—*like this is actually possible*, was a more confident way to think about what a Gap Year would look like. That was the framework I used to change my old way of thinking. In 2012, an adult time-out was not a real possibility for me, but by January 2013 it was, and the only thing I had changed was my rethinking possible. Rethinking possible turned an abstract idea into an incredible adult time-out. So every day I remind myself to Rethink Possible as I power on my BlackBerry.

12. Life Is a Mountain Not a Beach

How boring would life be if all we did was sit on a beach for fun? Don't get me wrong, I understand the saying about life and a beach with a cold beer—but really? A beach vacation is safe and involves little risk and no adventure. To me, it was similar to staying at the Firm and not taking an adult time-out (nor even risk asking for it). The safe way would have been to lay low and continue to go along with the flow of work, work, work and suck up all frustrations. Where is the fun and adventure in that? A man's mountain does not have to be Mount Everest, but we all need a climb and a challenge. There are things to do, see and be in life. I became motivated to live Big Law from a new altitude. Besides, life is better at the top.

13. Listen to Your Reservations and Move On

This step encourages you to become conscious of your decisions and minimizes the impulsive nature of decision-making. It is similar to Step 10—slow is smooth—but adds a listening element. My decision to take an adult time-out was not logical nor rational on many levels. There were many reservations about what this would cost me in the long run, both personally and professionally. But I was committed to being aware of and paying close attention to every reservation I had about my adult time-out. Reservations like *Will I lose all of my clients?*, *Will I lose all of my friends?* and *Will I be fired?* floated around my brain at that time. Listening to every reservation allowed me to become aware of what my concerns were, develop a plan around my reservations and be bold in making my Gap Period happen.

I was determined not to shortchange this experience. I formed a road map of whom I needed to speak with regarding my request, plus when and where my travels would take me. My reservations intensified as my planning unfolded. The reality of leaving work made me crazy at times. I had thoughts of *Lawyers in Big Law don't just up and leave and expect to return as if nothing transpired.* But on each occasion, I recognized and acknowledged each reservation, developed a plan to address them and implemented what some people may say was an irrational solution. Acknowledging even the slightest of reservation allowed me to blow past and get on with making my adult time-out happen.

These 13 steps were the foundation I used in developing a manuscript in asking for a Gap Year.

All courses of action are risky, so prudence is not in avoiding danger, but calculating risk and acting decisively. Make mistakes of ambition and not mistakes of sloth. Develop the strength to do bold things, not the strength to suffer.

—Niccolò Machiavelli, *The Prince*

CHAPTER THREE

MY MANUSCRIPT

Do you remember the scene from the movie *Jerry McGuire* when Tom Cruise, while sick, spent the night writing a manuscript about his vision for his sports agency firm? Jerry was moved, motivated and inspired to transform his company and more importantly, transform the way he served clients. The general theme of his manuscript was that one should have fewer clients, more client satisfaction and definitely more client attention. Before sunrise, he had the manuscript placed in each employee's inbox. When he woke, he had that *Oh s***, what did I do?* thought. He regretted handing out his manuscript but showed up at the office to a standing ovation by the entire staff. Two of his colleagues (supposedly friends) standing in the back, while smiling and clapping, questioned how long he would last before being fired. They figured he had a few days—and they were correct. A few days later, he was fired. Well, I wrote a similar manuscript to the managing partner of my Firm informing him that I was taking a Gap Period. And this is how it all went down.

As I returned home that late night in January of 2013 with the song "Behind Blue Eyes" still playing in my mind, I wrote a memorandum (my manuscript) to my Firm's managing partner with the intent of enrolling him in the idea that I was taking a Gap Year (in a telling type of way). It would be a year away from the accelerated pace and intensity of living life as a lawyer in Big Law. My manuscript was not a request—it was a notice, a statement, given in a polite and genuine manner, that I was stepping out of Big Law for a certain period of time.

In the history of my Firm, to my knowledge, taking a Gap Year had never been requested. This was a bold move. Instead of taking a break from law, most lawyers quit in frustration and join a competitor (where the cycle of frustration continues at the next firm down the street). I, however, did not want to quit nor leave my Firm. I simply wanted to slow the pace of my life for a short period of time and then hop back into the mix of Big Law.

In developing my manuscript, I anticipated that the managing partner had no idea what a Gap Year was (and I was right). My approach was to keep it simple, straightforward and assure him that I would return. I did not want my manuscript to sound like I needed a therapist (although I probably did), but rather, that I was a loyal Firm citizen in need of a break from my career.

I would like to report that words flowed onto my laptop in a stream of consciousness while drafting my manuscript, but that was not the case. The simple task of laying out what I really wanted and why proved challenging. My manuscript was not a list of complaints about the Firm, or other lawyers, or the possibilities of joining a competing law firm. These were not the reasons why I was taking a Gap Year. The manuscript was my sincere notice that I needed to take a break from the 47th floor. It was positive, genuine and forthright. I was emphatic that I could not imagine working at another Firm. I mentioned that my career had consumed my life, and I had become remarkably frustrated. I felt trapped in my own success as a lawyer. Something had to give. I was all in with my resolution to take a Gap Year. I was hoping the managing partner would recognize that allowing me a Gap Year would be simpler than having to hire a replacement. However, my need to take a Gap Year was so great that I was fully prepared to leave the Firm if my request was denied.

I also focused my manuscript on my commitment to take care of client emergencies as they arose, how I would be in dialogue with my clients before leaving and assuring clients that I would step in to resolve any issues that an associate was unable to handle. I explained how grateful, on a personal level, I was to the Firm for the last 25-plus years (i.e. being a partner had allowed me to send three kids to college and have each one graduate debt free).

I did not refer to any of my 13 Steps per se, but each one was a building block in the development of my manuscript. For example, I wrote about how:

1. My ERISA practice needed to evolve from historically generating fees through simple retirement plan drafting, compliance and litigation to areas within ERISA dealing with complex plan investing strategies and the like, and I needed to figure out how to make that happen. I also needed to see if I could trim my client base to focus on the 20 percent of clients that generated 80 percent of our revenue, create more and effective client engagement and finally, increase overall client service satisfaction for both the client and myself.

2. I could make the status quo work until age 65, but I had become curious how to make my legal career more expansive and thus make the Firm more prosperous.

3. A Gap Year, although unprecedented within the Firm, would make me a better lawyer, and the Firm would be better served if I took a break. I redefined taking a break as possible and that all three of us would win—clients, the Firm and myself.

4. I needed to grow as a lawyer in a way that did not fit the blueprint of the typical Firm partner and taking a Gap Year was the first step.

5. I wanted to transform my ERISA practice and make a career out of more than just billing hours, saving money in a 401(k) plan, retiring for a few years and then going ten toes up. I had convinced myself that there must be a different way to live life within the confines of the Firm, and I explained that I needed to figure out how to make it happen (he smiled understandingly when we spoke about how there must be a different way to live within the confines of Big Law. In fact, I believe I could see on his face a desire to also take a time-out).

I spoke with certain partners at the Firm regarding my decision to take a Gap Year. I was prepared to hear either a "good luck" (my positive and optimistic friends) or "you need to withdraw from the Firm because you have lost your mind" (my honest and pessimistic friends) or "we fully support you" but while smiling, really thinking I had lost my mind and I had better find a new job (my Jerry McGuire friends).[2]

The first person I spoke with was Susan (a positive and optimistic friend), a senior partner on the Firm's Executive Committee and an incredible lawyer. Susan and I had a good working relationship. We spent many long days on some exciting ERISA litigation matters, and I came to view her as a valued colleague and friend. When I told her that I was going to take a Gap Year, she said, "Great idea, I fully support your decision and will help out in any way possible in getting it approved." I felt absolutely triumphant. I sensed I was actually going to pull this Adventure off.

As we discussed my Gap Year (she had never heard this expression before), she questioned, "Why a year?" As I rationalized my thinking, she asked if I had thought about a shorter period of time, perhaps six months, and while we were discussing a six-month period, she

---

2 From the moment my Gap Period was approved through several months after my return, this group of friends became very resentful of my Adventure. These friends constantly asked, "Why you and not me?" I quickly exited these toxic friendships.

mentioned that women typically take four months for maternity leave and this seemed to refresh and energize them for when they return to the Firm. She also casually mentioned that she was about to take her family on a two-week vacation to South Africa and that she hadn't taken this much time off in years and was really looking forward to this break. She said that maybe I should take a short vacation and see how I felt when I came back before embarking on a year out of the Big Law game. *Maybe she is right*, I thought. Maybe a long weekend trip would shift my emotional tide of frustration. Following our conversation, I went to the gym feeling great and thinking that maybe a short vacation was all I really needed. It would definitely be less drastic.

It was not until later that afternoon I realized, s***—she just convinced me to change my plan from a Gap Year to a short vacation. One of my friends told me later that day, "Susan is good, she can convince a jury to her way of thinking, similar to how she convinced you to change your plans." Well, my eyes became wide open after that, and I was determined to stick to my original plan—or at least kind of, sort of.

The next person I spoke with was a 35-year career Firm partner. He had a brilliant legal mind, and clients from across the country lined up for his counsel. He was purely a numbers guy, in his early 60s and had a very old school mentality about work. He was the type that believed business casual was what one wore to the office on the weekends. I knew this conversation would be a good test to judge my commitment, resiliency and determination in taking a Gap Year.

As I walked into his office, I told him that I had something to tell him. From his facial expression, I sensed he was expecting me to say "I'm quitting." When I told him that I was not quitting but taking a Gap Year from the Firm, he was relieved, but at the same time, he did not "get" my Gap Year. At first, I thought I was not clear in articulating what I was doing and my reasons for taking this leave. I asked him, "Cal, do you ever wish that when you were 52 you had taken a year off just to see what life was all about?" I might as well have been speaking a different language to him. He said, "Of course not." He loved his career and had no reason to ever do something like that. I told him I would keep him posted, but as I left his office, I felt very unsupported. I needed a post-work run.

My final conversation was with Sean, the Firm's managing partner. Sean had recently been elected as the managing partner and was dealing with many Firm issues. I am positive he was not expecting nor liking the prospect of dealing with my Gap Year request. I had not worked much with Sean over the years, but he was an intelligent lawyer and knew how to deal with people issues and this certainly qualified as a "people issue."

I began the conversation by telling him a little bit about my life over the past 16 months. I explained my reasoning for taking a Gap Year and how I needed to step off the treadmill for a few months, take a break from my career and regain the edge to continue in Big Law. I also told him about the various offers I received from competing law firms and how I came to the conclusion that changing firms was not the solution to my funk (I'd like to think that he was relieved I was not changing firms). Overall, I focused on the *I just need to take a break* conversation. He interpreted this as I needed time to become rejuvenated about life again. I had not thought much about it in this "rejuvenating" my life way, but his thoughts and rationale were none of my business (see Step 1). I was doing what I needed. After we had spoken a bit longer, Sean thought a Gap Year was a great idea. He asked for my memorandum (my manuscript) setting forth my request, and he would discuss it with the Firm's Executive Committee.

In finalizing my manuscript, I decided to move my Gap Year to a period of four months plus two weeks, based on conversations with people whom I respected and who believed a four to six-month leave was more realistic. In retrospect, it was a huge mistake. Taking time off, no matter how long, including up to a year with a commitment to return was the correct decision, and I regret shortening my adult time-out. Changing my plan certainly violated Step 1 and was a reminder to always trust my instincts.

I delivered the manuscript to Sean on a Friday morning. The following Monday, Sean was in Houston and we spoke. It was a short and simple conversation. I was told to go recharge my batteries and come back ready to work. I assured him that I would let my clients know where I was and would handle all client-related issues as needed. This was the first time since I began my request that I felt truly supported. I was completely psyched. I felt as if the universe was really on my side.

Life can only be understood backwards; but it must be lived forwards.
—Søren Kierkegaard

PART II

MY ADULT TIME-OUT

CHAPTER FOUR

ON THE EDGE OF A NEW
TOMORROW

Most of us abandoned the idea of a life full of adventure and travel sometime between puberty and our first job. Our dreams died under the dark weight of responsibility. Occasionally the old urge surfaces, and we label it with names that suggest psychological aberrations: the big chill, a midlife crisis.

—Tim Cahill

Now that I received the green light, I began the planning phase. I wanted to begin my Adventure as a crew member on a sailboat from California to Hawaii. I researched this and quickly discovered there was an annual sailboat race from San Francisco to Hawaii that fit my time frame. After speaking with various yacht clubs in California, my plan was derailed. The yacht clubs I spoke with all thought this was a great idea and would certainly be an adventure, but because I had never been on a transoceanic sailboat, had never crewed before and did not know how to tie knots, it would be impossible to catch a ride. It was back to the drawing board.

As I sat in my den contemplating what now, I needed to think really hard about what did I want to do and accomplish during my Gap Period. *What did Mark want?* Although my primary goal was to unplug from Big Law, I also wanted some real adventure. A true out-of-the-box experience. I struggled with this *what does Mark want* question for a while. I had spent 25-plus years working and giving to clients and never made myself a priority. I really tried to think large and outside the norm. In my pre-working years, I had once read an article about container ships offering passengers the opportunity to travel on a working freighter, and so I set out to figure out how to catch a ride.

Thanks to Google, I quickly found a travel agency that specialized in freighter travel. This process was not exactly like booking on a Carnival Cruise Line where one's main concern was picking a dinner time and suite location. Mike, the freighter travel agent I spoke with, scruffily said that he would be able to assist me and would mail out information. I asked if he could email it instead, and he abruptly said, "No, it will be sent to your house."

Okay…

The material arrived a few days later, and I found a passage from Newark to various ports in the Mediterranean. I decided I would take the 29-day voyage from Newark to Genoa, Italy and then head to Africa.

I called Mike the following day to check availability. In his gruff-like way, he said he would get back to me in a few days. Before hanging up, I asked him, "Have you ever taken one of these container ships?" Without hesitation, Mike answered, "Hell no. Why would I do something like that?" He suggested I consider a shorter trip before being stuck all by myself on a container ship for 29 days. His comments in no way dampened my enthusiasm for a trans-Atlantic container ship experience.

A few days later, Mike called and informed me there was an open bed (I was not sure what this looked like—a bunk room with a bunch of sailors was my first thought) on a ship leaving Newark on May 5th making stops in Virginia, Georgia, Spain, Malta and Italy. He also said I had 48 hours to pay in full for a non-refundable, one-way ticket without being allowed to review paperwork or any other documents regarding the trip. Now being a lawyer, that was really difficult, but I thought, *What the hell, my Adventure was already beginning.*

The following day I overnighted a check to Mike and received my paperwork two weeks later with confirmation that I had a bed aboard the CMA CGM Jamaica—my home for 29-plus days (the exact arrival date in Italy was subject to change).

Planning My Journey

Now that I was set for my trip out of the USA, I needed to plan for the post-container ship part of my Adventure. South Africa had always fascinated me ever since my first trip there in 2012 for work. The client spoke with such passion about Cape Town, the Garden Route and the Wild Coast. He raved about Cape Town's great food and wine. I decided this would be my first African stop. Following this stop, I decided to drive up the east coast to Durban and then into Mozambique, Uganda, Kilimanjaro and then back to Europe to visit Italy and France, and then home. My goal was to travel most of this by train and/or bus. The desire was short lived, however, when I recognized that it would take an immense amount of time to travel throughout Africa over land (and may not be safe).

While planning my South Africa visit, I contacted a local running club in Cape Town, who gave me some great suggestions on where to stay. More importantly, they invited me for a run when I arrived. Running clubs are an awesome way to meet people. In the fall of 2011 I joined a local Houston running club and met some amazing people. This Houston running club would meet every Wednesday night at six for a six-mile run and then go to a bar at Rice University and drink $1 beers. Then every Friday they went to a happy hour at some local dive bar. Running and drinking beer—what a great group of people.

I remember my first Wednesday night run. It was in mid-December. I showed up around 5:45 for the 6:00 start. I noticed four women and thought, *They can't be that fast.* Boy, was I wrong. One woman was legally blind and another was an Italian hairdresser, and they both ran 3:15 marathons (which is an hour faster than my time). The other two were not much slower. I kept up with them for about three miles when one said that she would slow down and lead me to the bar. While I did my best to hang with the group while running, I did much better keeping up with them during the beer drinking.

As I was making my travel plans, my daughter went to the hospital and gave birth to my first grandson. I had plenty of time on delivery day to research flight options and make bookings while she was in labor. I was hoping United and its Star Alliance member airlines would make this a simple exercise, though, it was easier said than done.

United and South African Airlines would get me to most places. I had to book a local airline, Precision Air, in and out of Uganda. This made me somewhat nervous since neither the travel agent nor myself had ever heard of this carrier. I was able to book a ride on Ethiopian Airlines out of Kilimanjaro and Air France into Bordeaux. I booked my flight home on good ole United. Now the game was truly on!

Only those who will risk going too far can possibly find out how far one can go.
—T.S. Eliot, Preface to Harry Crosby's *Transit of Venus*

CHAPTER FIVE

LET ADVENTURE 2013 BEGIN

Only put off until tomorrow what you are willing to die having left undone.
—Pablo Picasso

My Final Day at Work

I arrived on the 47th floor at my normal 7 a.m. starting time. For the most part, I kept busy finishing up some last minute projects, assigning projects to my associates and not to mention putting in a full day of billable hours. I decided to call my Gap Period a "working sabbatical" to clients (this terminology sounded politically correct at the time, but in hindsight, I'm not sure it reflected what I did exactly). The majority of my clients understood my need to take a Gap Period, but there is always one, and one in particular, who thought I would be better off playing a couple rounds of golf at a fancy golf course in Arizona to shake things off.

I had no idea how I would feel as my final day in the office came to an end, but I must have entered the elevator lobby at least five times before actually getting in and staying on the elevator. As I pressed the M button and began to descend, an incredible emotion came over me. Strange thoughts raced through my head like: *I have done this ERISA work for almost 26 years, and that is more than enough; there is life outside the Firm; I have just quit my job and I am never coming back.* Time slowed as I passed each floor, and with each floor passed, I began to feel my shoulders relax more and more. An unexplainable lightness of relief was felt within my soul as I headed to the ground floor. Happiness shone on my face and in my smile as the door opened, an emotion that had long since been buried by all of those billable hours. An internal freedom burst within me as I exited the elevator, something I had never experienced before, and it made me so much more excited for what was to come as I walked to my car.

Over the next two days, my conversations with friends about my journey turned into anticipation of *what will Mark be like when he returns to Houston?* I had not really thought about that much, but just thinking about this question flooded my brain with ideas on how I should live the next 25 or so years of my life. Will I return to the Firm and continue to draft retirement plans, litigate retirement plan issues and otherwise reproduce what I had done for the past 25-plus years? Or will I move in a different direction? For the first time in my adult life, I was freeing myself from the programmed life I created. I truly felt I had been given a second chance, or did I create an opportunity to begin a new life, with a clean slate?

The Eve of My Adventure

Fear isn't only a guide to keep us safe; it's also a manipulative emotion that can trick us into living a boring life…the great stories go to those who don't give in to fear.
—Donald Miller, *A Million Miles in a Thousand Years: What I Learned While Editing My Life*

What the f*** have I done with my life? Am I totally messing up a great legal career? As I sat in the den of my house on the eve of my Adventure, the overarching feeling I had was fear. A fear as if I was in the process of f***ing up my entire life and career by taking this Adventure. I began to think that rational and right-minded people just don't do what I was about to do. I really thought I was making a muck out of a pretty successful and comfortable life.

However, in those fleeting moments of calm, rationality and excitement, I was hoping that by taking this Adventure (a) my kids would see it as an example that they too could take a break from corporate America and not totally ruin a career and (b) my action would inspire some successful person sitting behind a big mahogany desk wearing a suit to take a break—not quit or change jobs or careers—but simply take an adult time-out. I was the test case to see if this experiment could work.

The Ride to the Airport

Departure day arrived. I was anxious, nervous and excited all at the same time. This Gap Period thing was actually happening!

My daughter drove me to the airport, and shortly after getting on the highway, I broke down in tears. I couldn't help but think about work, my family and that I was most likely in the process of f***ing everything up that I spent the last 25 years creating. The emotion of leaving Houston, the Firm and my life finally caught up with me. My daughter began to cry too and told me how much I meant to her throughout her pregnancy and the birth of her son and that she could not have done it without me. It was a special moment that will always live in my heart. All that had mattered to me for so long was to be a family man, a good father. This is really who I was, who I still am, and I told her that I would always be there for her and my two sons.

Despite all the tears we shed, I made it to the airport in one piece. We gave each other a long hug, and I watched her drive off through the tears in my eyes. I said to myself, "Let the Gap Period begin," as I headed to the gate.

He went to Paris looking for answers to questions that bothered him so… married an actress…they had a good life…20 years slipped away…hopped on a freighter, skidded the ocean and left…without a sound.
                                        —Jimmy Buffet, *He Went to Paris*

CHAPTER SIX

THE CONTAINER SHIP EXPERIMENT: UNPLUGGING

Peace be with you...And with your spirit...And protect me from all anxiety as I go...

—Rite of Peace at a Roman Catholic Mass

My sole purpose in taking the Adventure was to unplug from Big Law for four-plus months. Although this seemed like a simple goal, I had serious doubts as to whether I could actually make this happen. I hoped the solitary confinement of a container ship would give me the best chance to truly unplug. So, I treated the Atlantic crossing as an experiment to see whether I could make unplugging actually happen.

Before leaving for Newark to board the container ship, I went to the 7 a.m. Mass at St. Patrick's Cathedral in New York City to ask God, his angels and his saints to protect me on this Adventure, especially from anxiety. The priest preached on how one finds peace easily when all is calm, but must strive to find peace in the midst of chaos. He gave the example of the Boston Marathon bombings and discussed how one can find peace and be peaceful even in the middle of terrible destruction. This homily put me in a great state of mind for my Adventure: remain in a peaceful state of mind despite my out-of-control thoughts and feelings with leaving work for four-plus months, traveling for 29 days on a container ship full of sailors and then spending two months in Africa, all on a shoestring. This message of staying peaceful in the midst of what I was feeling (aka *what am I doing with my life?*) couldn't have been more timely.

During Mass, I needed to remind myself that what I really wanted to accomplish was to unplug from the legal billing machine that drove me to the point of needing a break, to unplug from the stress of a complex and sophisticated Big Law ERISA practice, managing client relations, managing associates and billing in tenths of an hour for a required minimum eight hours per day, all the while trying to find some time to get in a run for a few miles without feeling guilty for having some *me* time. I felt trapped and imprisoned in a career that I created. Deep within my soul, I really had no intention of walking away from a career that I truly enjoyed and had provided me with so much. I just wanted to step off the legal treadmill, live life and focus on my career from a different dimension and then re-emerge once again into Big Law. While kneeling in my pew, eyes closed and hands clenched in prayer, I felt as though the priest was speaking directly to me. He was feeding my soul with what I needed to hear.

Following Mass, I caught a shiny black Town Car from my New York hotel and asked the driver to take me to the shipyards in Jersey. He had never taken a passenger to the shipyards, and thanks to his Garmin, we were able to find the security gate. Now Jersey union longshoremen are a rare breed and in no way look or act like a United check-in agent. As I approached the security gate guy with my paperwork, he looked at me and said, "I have never seen or heard of anyone having a ticket for a container ship," and when I handed him my ticket, he again responded that he had never seen one—ever. Boy, was I feeling great at this point. He truly had no clue who I was or what I was doing.

The guard made a few calls on how to process me through a chain-link security gate. His buddy drove up in a beat-up pickup truck with a New Jersey Port Authority seal stamped on the car door. Picture this: a 64-year-old crusty longshoreman who probably smokes a few packs a day picking up a guy with a backpack and a guitar (yes, I brought my guitar with the hopes of learning more than "This Old Man") who was just dropped off by a fancy, shiny black Town Car. His buddy would drive me to where the ship was docked but said, "You ain't goin' aboard without permission from the captain." I thought, *how the hell was I going to get on the boat?* He asked whether this was my first time, and I explained I had not been on *any* boat before this one. He very quickly explained in a gruff-like tone that, "Boats can go on ships but ships can't go on boats, and you should learn the difference." At that moment, all I wanted to do was get on that ship. He proceeded to ask me if I had ever been up the gangway. Of course, I had not, and he said, "Them there are not steps but funny round things, and you better hold on to the rails carefully." Well, this advice was taken once I started up the gangway—one could easily break an ankle on those round looking steps. I actually contemplated not leaving the ship until arriving in Italy!

I reached the top of the gangway and presented my passport and paperwork to an official-looking person, and was processed as a passenger into the container ship's computer system. I was relieved my paperwork was in order. A crew member led me to my room via an elevator to floor G. I was surprised the container ship had an elevator and that there were ten floors. As for my room, it was not a room full of bunk beds to be shared with a bunch of smelly, sweaty sailors as I had imagined. Instead, it was a private two-room "suite" (well sort of) with windows looking straight up the middle of the ship. A major worry was relieved.

After a little bit of exploring, I made a few calls, finished up some last minute projects (which I resented doing and took as a sign that I was ready to unplug from Big Law) and spoke with a few friends before departure. As I was talking with them, that Jerry McGuire feeling of totally messing up my life roared through my consciousness. Even though I was being told what I was doing was

great and a few "I'm proud of you" statements were made, I did not
fully believe or embrace them. However, I was determined to get
off the grid—Jason Bourne style—and see what happened. On a
more positive and uplifting thought, I felt as if I was becoming the
most interesting person (or at least the most talked about person)
within the halls of the Firm.

Before nightfall, I returned a call from a client who had some
last minute questions on their company's pension plan. After we
had talked some "ERISA speak" dealing with actuarial funding
issues (I always wanted to be an actuary and found this stuff very
interesting), we spoke about my Adventure. She is one of the 99
percent of my clients (remember the one who told me all I should
do is go play a couple rounds of golf at a nice resort) who had
embraced this Adventure of mine. I told her that my number one
goal was to unplug from Big Law, and she immediately understood
and asked for my blog site (myadulttimeout.com). Later that night,
she responded as follows:

> I found it! I read your first posts and look forward
> to seeing the photos once you post them. Enjoy this
> JOURNEY, Mark.
>
> You will be missed!
>
> Best,
> Sharon

This simple email put me in one of the greatest moods and had
me looking forward to what's to come. As I sat in my room settling
into my first day on the CMA CGM Jamaica, I realized there was no
comparison between waiting to depart from the docks of the Jersey
shore to waiting in the United Club with stressed out, overweight
business people in suits, drinks in hand and staring at a flight monitor
that most likely indicated a flight delay. I couldn't help but think as I
drifted off to sleep—this was truly living life differently.

I Hope I Don't Fall Overboard!

I received the "official" safety tour of the container ship from my tour guide, Albert. Although my room and the dining areas were spotless, this ship was definitely not governed by US Safety Rules and Regulations. The life rafts/boats/preservers appeared to have not been touched since they were installed. They had become cemented to the sides and floors through built-up rust. The path around the container ship had a foot wide red line, and I was told to walk it whenever I was on deck. That was pretty easy since a mountain of containers stacked ten high were a foot to your right and a three-foot railing to keep one (me) from falling overboard was a foot to your left. Yes, you read right, *only* a three-foot railing to keep me from falling into the ocean only ten feet below the deck.

Loading and unloading.

According to Albert, passengers enjoyed getting out of their rooms and stretching their legs by going for a "walkabout"—but casually cautioned it was best to do this with calm seas. Smirkingly, he mentioned it took passengers a few days to develop the courage to go outside. My only thought was that I probably would never experience walking that red line.

On this tour, Albert showed me all of the container ship's amenities. In no way are the amenities on a container ship similar to those on a Carnival Cruise Line. The container ship had a gym consisting of a ping pong table, a very old elliptical machine (which sort of worked) and a sauna I had no intention of ever using. There was a 12 by 12 by 12 foot indoor pool I was told they would fill once the ship left US jurisdiction. Albert had no response to my question about the timing of filling the pool, but like the sauna, I had no interest in a swim while at sea. However, the pool area did have a heavy punching bag which I used during my daily workouts. And finally, on the same floor as my room, there was a second gym, a room consisting of a smattering of free weights and a machine that had most of its parts missing.

Doing What I Want—A First for Me!

As I began the journey of unplugging, I had a stark realization that on this Adventure I would get to do exactly what I wanted, when I wanted. This was a first for me. I was pumped! It was just me on a container ship with 20 crew members who spoke very little English. A great setting for an introvert.

A REFLECTIVE MOMENT: As a lawyer in today's world of Big Law, your career is your way of life. One has a responsibility to maintain contact with clients and make sure their issues are taken care of immediately so that clients do not look to other firms for assistance. Vacations were, in reality, a futile attempt of unplugging from the billing machine. The experiment of unplugging made me reflect on my past vacations. Ultimately, the goal of all vacations is to unplug, rewind and get some relaxation, but in reality, I never came close to unplugging from Big Law. It was not until I was on a container ship with approximately 4,000 steel crates, traveling across the Atlantic Ocean, having no communication with the Firm or clients, did I realize that for the past 25-plus years I had never truly unplugged. While I was on the ocean, I had no idea what was going on at the Firm, in the stock market, the world, the Middle East, on Fox News or at the White House. Even if I wanted to make contact, I wasn't able to. All I knew was nothing other than the dark blue water and large bright sun in front of me. It was such a fantastic feeling. This was the true meaning of unplugging.

"The Boys Are Back in Town"

After two days at sea, the container ship was making its first stop in Norfolk, VA. I woke to the sound of horns and flashing lights at 3 a.m., and I was very excited to see land. It was a Christopher

Columbus moment. I was not quite sure why I was excited to get off the container ship, but I had my departure pass in hand, and after a quick breakfast with the captain, who reminded me that we would sail between 6:00 and 8:00 that night, I was off. The crew had arranged for a taxi (this particular cab driver was always waiting at port for the ship to come in) to take me around. I felt like a regular merchant marine with a six-hour shore pass. The captain had mentioned most passengers head to the local mall as it was a short ride from the docks. Once I was processed through the port's version of Homeland Security (basically showing a badge that I was a passenger on the ship) and knowing nothing else about Norfolk other than I wanted to be near the ship, I asked the driver, Lisa, to head for the Norfolk mall.

I arrived just as the doors to the mall were opening and experienced something completely unexpected. Stores had not even pulled up their metal gates when I was nearly trampled by all the senior citizens walking up and down the mall, cruising with their headsets blaring pop music (I'm sure their grandkids programmed this for them) getting in their daily cardio. They were everywhere, dressed in colorful Lululemon outfits and super nice looking tennis shoes and walking with such determination. This was by no means a social hour for these retirees—it was purely business.

When I returned to the ship, I had various work projects pop up on my BlackBerry. It was an indicator that I was still far from being unplugged. In fact, the act of unplugging turned out to be more of a journey than a destination. But my self-imposed solitary confinement served as an inspiration for me to make the experiment of unplugging happen.

When speaking with associates and other partners on various projects, I felt like Jerry McGuire in the scene where he sings "Free Falling" with a smile on his face not realizing that he was, in fact, in a free fall with his career, friends and family. I wondered if I was Jerry and in an emotional free fall. I went from working daily in a fancy office that served Starbucks to a container ship where no one spoke English and the coffee was dark, thick and oh so strong. I was determined to stay conscious in my fall from a successful Big Law career if that was how this turned out.

Meals on a Container Ship

I quickly learned meals aboard the container ship were simply more of the same. Lunch consisted of soup, salad, rice and cold (and often old looking) shrimp or chicken. For dinner, it seemed we always had a version of chicken noodle soup similar to the one we had at lunch. I use the term *version* because at each meal (lunch and dinner), the menu would state "chicken noodle soup" but the color of the soup would drastically change. The taste, however, was the same. The only difference between the lunch and dinner versions was that the dinner chicken noodle soup stayed on the stove for an additional five hours (to thicken up and change to a dark green in color). The soup of the day became something that I looked forward to each day. I was always curious how dark the soup could turn between lunch and dinner. On the upside, there was always a nice bottle of red wine for both lunch and dinner. Breakfast consisted of an egg and what the cook referred to as "sausage." The sausage was an American hot dog fried in a pan instead of boiled in a pot, and after 29 days of hot dogs for breakfast, I hoped to never see one again.

We are all brothers and sisters.
—Captain Alex from the CMA CGM Jamaica (describing the relationship between the people of the Ukraine and Russia)

The captain was in his mid-40s, about five feet five inches tall and about 50 pounds overweight. He was always polite, spoke broken English and was a no-bulls*** type of person who barely smiled. I could tell he was all about rules and regulations (and did not like many of them). He made a point that "they"—the rules—would be followed at all times with no exceptions. For example, there would be no impromptu visits to the bridge; all visits required an invitation—by him.

When I first met him, he enthusiastically told me about his visit to Victoria's Secret while the ship was loading/unloading in Newark. He was very excited about what he purchased. I assumed it was for his wife but based on the conversations we had—I could not be certain. He repeatedly said, "I can't buy these costumes in Kiev." As we talked, I could not resist asking his opinion on the effects of the breakup of the Soviet Union. In his opinion, and that of his family and friends, it was not that big of a deal. He stated, "We are all brothers and sisters." To him, he and the Ukraine were still part of the Soviet Union (very prophetic back in 2013).

A REFLECTIVE MOMENT: The captain's comment on how we are all brothers and sisters hit a cord. It had me wondering: if Big Law operated as a family, would it become more profitable, meaning—if Firm lawyers worked better with one another, would we generate more business together than on our own? I believe there is a fine line between cooperation and discord among lawyers, similar to brothers and sisters, and cooperation amongst lawyers in the same Firm results in a surplus of profits, while discord results in fewer profits for the firm. It's a small degree of separation but a huge disparity when it comes to making money. What I had yet to figure out was how to harmonize cooperation and limit discord within the confines of Big Law. Nevertheless, I do know that grouping for client origination credit is the single most counterproductive activity that Big Law lawyers stress over. Big Law needs to focus first and foremost on attaining and serving clients with exceptional service and leave the origination credit for another day. I was determined to bring exceptional service to my fellow partners and their clients. Exceptional comradery among partners would benefit all those involved: the client, my partners and me included.

The three other Ukrainian officers were your stereotypical Eastern European type—blonde hair, square jaws. They rarely spoke, even when engaged. They came and went from the dining area very quickly, often taking their food with them when they left. I had no intention of getting on their bad side because shore was a long way off. One afternoon, I had a ping pong game with the chief electrician, who was also the ship's barber. He was super intense and did not like losing (which he graciously did). On Saturdays, he would have a line of crew waiting for a haircut in the gym area.

After a week of cruising the Atlantic Seaboard, we headed to our final port in the USA, Savannah. We were picking up a new passenger for the trip across the Atlantic. I was hoping it might be someone like Kate Upton, but according to the crew, most passengers are on a mission trip. I thought that if he was on a mission trip, he might be Mormon, and we could laugh about the Broadway musical *Book of Mormon* and discuss the songs "Just Turn It Off" and the "Scary Mormon Hell Dream."

A REFLECTIVE MOMENT: Looking out at the bluest water that my blue eyes had ever seen, I came to realize that the success of Big Law is premised on lawyers keeping their heads down, cranking out an incredible amount of billable hours and otherwise going along passively with management. This was my work ethic for the past 25-plus years. It was neither right nor wrong, but rather, the way Big Law works.

As my Adventure unfolded, I realized I could not unplug by simply turning a knob. It became a constant emotional struggle between the solitude of the Atlantic Ocean and the racket of work, clients and attorneys occupying my every thought. As each day passed (and each time zone crossed), I was beginning to see obstacles in my work life (for example, the speed of each day), and for the first time in my life, I knew I had a choice to stop the insanity of Big Law. I recalled Johnny Nash's song lyrics *I can see clearly now the rain has gone. I can see all obstacles in my way.* It seems like too many people (including me) get stuck in their obstacles rather than walking around the issue to clearer skies. Who cares why there is an obstacle? How much better off is one when he/she understands "it"? When our ship approached a storm (obstacle), Captain Alex mentioned that he could stay the course and go directly into the storm and deal with the stress on the crew (and passengers), ship and cargo and deal with all the repercussions, or he could sidestep it by going around the storm and stay in the clear and calm waters where everyone is happy and content. I became determined to quickly move beyond my obstacles in life without getting bogged down in the hows and whys of them.

A REFLECTIVE MOMENT: Big Law has a different definition of a work/life balance. Work is your life. But billing hours often breeds regrets in lawyers as they climb the Big Law ladder of illusionary success. In taking my time-out, I clearly saw an imbalance. Few partners who reach retirement are happy at this supposed great juncture in their working lives. Most regret not having had more fun during their working years, and most are too physically worn down to actualize their dreams of an adventurous retirement. In my heart, I believe that most lawyers spend far too many hours being ambitious about the wrong things. I have come across this many times with partners while assisting them in filling out their retirement paperwork. It seems most of these meetings are paradoxical—resentment and happy feelings as each box is checked off on the pension paperwork.

Before I left on my Adventure, I spoke with a lawyer friend who, after being a loyal Firm citizen at another Big Law firm for 38 long, hardworking years, was being forced to retire at the age of 61. While helping him fill out his pension application, he mentioned that actuarially he had only 15 more years to live, and he should have traded in some of those hard 38 years for more retirement years. A sad commentary on the life of a partner in Big Law. I did not want to live that way. I did not want to have any regrets. I did not want to become that lawyer.

Going forward, when a potential new hire has a question on our Firm's work/life balance, I would hope the Firm would direct them to me where I can prove to them that there can be a way to accomplish balance without allowing the seeds of resentment to sprout.

Leaving the USA

Before we left the docks at Savannah, I had a very busy day dealing with work issues. It was another data point on the unplugging spectrum that demonstrated to my psyche that I was far from being disconnected to Big Law. I was, however, entering a period of 12 consecutive days of crossing the Atlantic Ocean where there would be absolutely no BlackBerry service. I was really going off the grid (and I was welcoming it).

A REFLECTIVE MOMENT: Big Law seems to produce lawyers who become subject to what I refer to as the "puppy chow syndrome" (PCS). PCS is my version of the following: I give associates work to do. They mostly get it done correctly, and when they show up for work the following day, mysteriously, there is more work. They rarely ask questions as a follow-up to an assignment given. They simply expect more work. Associates seldom ask about the history of the client, how the client came to the Firm, if the Firm does other work for a particular client or how can the Firm expand its representation of that client. It is akin to a puppy and its food. Each morning its bowl is full of food to eat, and the puppy is never concerned with how it got there. This is PCS. This is the state of the modern day Big Law associate. Where is the service in that? Whether giving service at a restaurant or a lawyer to a client, great service will always generate return business. This is true even if the cost of the service is expensive (or the food is not that good). People remember service! Big Law must encourage (require) associates to engage with clients on a level beyond completing projects and billing hours.

Nothing Matters Much, and Much Does Not Matter

Far from a supermodel, my shipmate, Nicholas, was a retired high school teacher from a select private school in Carmel, CA. He taught French, Greek and some type of classical art. I got the impression he was the type of teacher who probably never gave a solid A to a student. Nicholas was a veteran of around-the-world travel without the aid of an airplane, and this was not his first rodeo on a container ship. He had taken many container ships from various ports throughout the world and enjoyed the pace of this type of travel. After dinner on his first night, he asked that I give him a tour of the inside of the ship, and I gladly did. I felt like a cruise director showing him around—as if I actually knew the ship. We stopped by the gym, pool and sauna as well as some other areas I had recently discovered (the crew lounge and the lounge reserved for officers). The officers' lounge consisted of a wooden card table, an empty bar and an area where you could watch DVDs on a 1970 two-hundred-pound looking television. Lastly, I showed him my newly discovered outside sitting area on the G deck. This place was a 12 by 16 foot area where I read, wrote and played a little guitar when the weather was nice.

Getting to know people just does not happen very often with me. As I set out to cross the Atlantic, I decided I really wanted to get to know Nicholas. Generally, when I meet someone new, I quickly find out where they work, what school(s) they attended and whether we have any acquaintances in common. Superficial at best and, in the back of my mind, I'm always thinking how that person could become a client or refer business at some future time. This time, I wanted to be free of that way of thinking and find out who this person *really* was.

Nicholas was traveling to meet up with his brother who was to perform in a concert in Italy. He had never been married and had no kids. However, he had lots of cousins and enjoyed seeing his former students, especially the foreign exchange ones while on his travels.

During breakfast one morning, I asked him, "What are some life lessons you have learned?" After a chuckle, he stated, "I do not live that way." I wasn't sure what he meant by that, but he continued to say "Mark, don't be in a hurry." Now being on a container ship cured me of being in a hurried state of mind but he meant it at a deeper level. I believe he was saying it as a way of life, a way of thinking and a way of being each and every day. I'm sure this is what every yoga teacher aspires to achieve with his/her yoga practice. And, to me, Nicholas had achieved a "no hurry" state of being. I, on the other hand, had not.

Nicholas, with a smile on his face, also said, "Nothing matters much, and much does not matter at all." He asked me to think about this as he left the breakfast table. I sat finishing my coffee, reflecting on what he just said and came to agree with him. Big Law and its illusion of significance really does not mean much in the big picture of life. Big Law, although it offered me a great career, was just a means to financially facilitate a comfortable and secure life.

A REFLECTIVE MOMENT: One afternoon while sitting outside overlooking the ocean, I questioned why so much success had driven me to the verge of a life away from the 47th floor. I knew there was no true and straightforward answer to this, and I quickly rid myself of trying to find a sensible explanation and instead enjoyed a peaceful and calm day at sea.

Mother's Day

It was a beautiful Mother's Day on the Atlantic Ocean. The day was sunny, the water a bit choppy, and I enjoyed watching the containers sway from side to side. How they all stayed onboard was surprisingly amazing considering there were no apparent restraints to hold down any of the 4,000 containers. Holidays away from family are never easy for me, especially Mother's Day. My mom is such a great supporter,

especially of my Adventure, and as the sun rose in the east, I could not help but reflect on how good she has been to me for so many years (in fact, my entire life ☺). Not being able to call her was certainly a downside to being electronically unplugged.

An early morning at sea.

Mother's Day also meant that we were greeted at breakfast with pancakes instead of the normal eggs and hot dogs—I mean sausage. The pancakes had a taste like no other pancake—all in a good way. In fact, it was so good I had a second one. Following breakfast, Nicholas and I ordered a case of Heineken beer. The container ship had a "slopshop" where passengers and crew members could purchase

Having dinner with (left to right) the captain, electrician and Nicholas.

all sorts of goods from popcorn (a favorite for the Ukrainians) to candy, soda and shaving items. It was the container ship's version of a hotel gift store, but only passengers were allowed to purchase beer and wine. We decided to split a case for some pre-dinner drinks. Items were sold in US dollars and were listed on a sheet of paper posted on the wall in the dining area. After placing our beer order with the cook, the case mysteriously appeared in my cabin later that afternoon.

As it turned out, Nicholas was quite fond of beer. Our pre-dinner beers turned into afternoon beers as well as post-dinner beers while watching the sunset. Our conversations on the G deck, with a beer in hand, became a time of day that I looked forward to. We would get on all kinds of topics ranging from travel, to family, to even politics. These conversations in no way reflected the substance of my conversations around the water cooler back on the 47th floor. They ran a little deeper. Nicholas is a wise man and his observations and ability to articulate views always had me thinking.

Mother's Day was also the day the crew had their "crossing the Atlantic" celebratory cookout. The crew put on a BBQ for the officers, Nicholas and me. They barbecued some type of squid and meat that looked disgusting but tasted great. They cleared an outside deck, and we all sat at a long table and had a great supper (I

chose a chair with my back against the wall as opposed to the light
rail with an ocean on the other side). It was the only time that we all
ate together. It was fun to interact with everyone as we watched the
sunset over the Atlantic. That night the crew descended to the crew
lounge for movie night, and I was invited. Well, the movies were
in English with Filipino subtitles, but with these types of movies,
subtitles were not necessary (and the movies did not involve Bruce
Lee), so I did not stay long.

A REFLECTIVE MOMENT: I was finishing up my current read
about a guy dragging his wife and young kids to India so he could
find the ever elusive concepts called peace, love and happiness (as
if peace, love and happiness are tangible things that can be located).
We all want these concepts, but this read got me thinking about my
own happiness when it comes to my career. I decided that I needed to
establish more happiness in my work life. To make it a priority. I know
one cannot be completely happy without some disappointment, but
I intended not to sacrifice happiness for living, and wanting to live,
in a certain way. I will work the way I want to work and not how it's
historically been done, according to the unspoken code of Big Law.[3]
Simply billing hours was no longer a way to live life, at least not for
me. An endless hour-by-hour approach did not sit well with clients
either. Billing hours had become a slow death to my soul. Realizing
how my soul was deteriorating with each hour billed, I seriously
began to contemplate not returning to Big Law. I was approaching
the proverbial "edge" of concluding Big Law was inconsistent with
how I wanted to live out my remaining working years. I questioned
whether continuing my career was merely deceiving myself that the
glory and prestige of Big Law were more valuable to me than pursuing
my true essence as an adventurous soul.

The possibility of not returning made the thought of drafting
401(k) plans inconsequential, especially while looking out over the
bluest water with a glass of Italian red wine in the middle of the

---

3 The code: billing the most hours one possibly can at the highest hourly rate.

Atlantic Ocean. At that moment, I felt I was really moving into a new phase of my life, a new direction, and I was pumped.

Changes in Latitudes,
Changes in Attitudes—Jimmy Buffett

Six days into the Atlantic crossing I woke with a jolt of fear running through my body as I flew off my bed. We were caught in a major Atlantic storm, and the container ship was being tossed around like I never imagined a ship as large as I was on could be tossed. I was in complete fear. I felt I was going to actually die as the waves crashed onto the ship. Sirens rang and lights flashed as the ship's speakers were telling people who knows what in Ukrainian. I would have kneeled in prayer, but that was an impossibility as I was thrown against the walls. I had no clue how many tons a container ship weighed when you add 4,000 containers carrying what I assumed was mostly crap from China, but the container ship was no match for this mighty Atlantic storm.

Everything on my desk, including my iPad, was being tossed around on the floor. Even my rosary ended up on the floor under a heap of stuff. My closet was completely empty when the sun rose and the seas calmed. My clothes were everywhere. I was certain many of the containers were hopping somewhere in the ocean. After three long hours, the storm calmed down. It was almost 4 a.m., and it took a while to calm my racing heart as I sat on the side of my bed with my hands clenched in prayer. At that moment, I was convinced I totally, as a matter of rational fact, f***ed up my entire life.

Besides worrying that the container ship almost sank, I thought that my work life was not that bad and escaping on a container ship with 20 men, who spoke very little English, was a total and monumental mistake in judgment on my part. At that moment, I felt I should have just gutted out my frustrations with work, kept my head down and stayed the course until my normal retirement age.

At breakfast that morning, the captain said the ship had no way to avoid the storm, but thankfully it sustained no real damage, and no containers were lost. He also said that we were prohibited from going outside until the crew secured the containers and made sure that all was protected on deck. I had no issues complying with his mandate.

The necessity of setting the world at a distance from us, when we are to take a survey of ourselves, has sent many from high stations to the severities of a monastic life.

—Samuel Johnson, *The Rambler* No. 23

Nicholas and I were having lunch one afternoon when he shared the quote above from a book he was reading. It was a collection of periodicals written by Samuel Johnson in the 1750s called *The Rambler*. Now I had no intentions of becoming a monk or moving into a monastery, but stepping back and taking a survey of my work life (while living a solitary life on a ship) made me think this Adventure was becoming a transition period. I began to consider questions like: *Do I want to stay at the Firm? Do I want to move to a smaller firm? Do I want to work on project-only assignments? Do I want to completely move away from law altogether?* It became very clear I did not want to become one of those Firm partners who reached his/her 65th birth date and realized the Firm was forcing him/her out. In my role as Chair of the Retirement Plan Committee, I have worked with too many partners who do not understand that the partnership is a big business and if you are not productive, you just cannot stay around, but boy, do they try. The unproductive partners have all kinds of rationalizations on "why the Firm needs me." For example, "I'm the only partner who knows local easement law" and "I'm the only partner who has the relationship with ABC Corporation, a $1,000,000 a year client," which usually turns out to be a $10,000 a year client. I have heard all of the rationalizations.

A REFLECTIVE MOMENT: There is so much more to me than being an ERISA lawyer. Sure the pay is great and I get to work on complex and sophisticated projects, but being on the container ship made me realize I had evolved as a person. I pondered if it was time to move on. I knew that I wanted to be bold and take some risks, especially over the next 25 years or so (hoping that God grants me extra innings). Thoughts of merely repeating the past for the coming years had become depressing and unacceptable to me.

Scary Mormon Hell Dream

Thank you for your years of service, Mark, but we no longer need you. I am sorry, Mark. We are going to have to let you go. No, not me—they promised I could stay until the end of the year! Was I in denial?

I awoke one night to this miserable dream. I wondered whether I had become one of those partners who was not aware that he had become unproductive, or was there a bit of reality with my Jerry McGuire friends in that there was no room within Big Law for adult time-outs? Maybe Susan, and to some degree Cal, were inferring that it was time for me to move my career in a new direction and I missed their subtle message. Obviously, I did not like waking up to this, but I was seriously considering whether Big Law was still right for me. While thinking about Big Law, I realized that when I was at work, I was not authentic 90 percent of the time—being who I truly was behind these blue eyes. I hid my adventurous self. My internal light was not only dimmed, it had turned off. Blue Eyes had evolved into a successful Firm partner, but the person behind those blue eyes was not showing up and expressing himself. I questioned whether that person would be able to continue to "work" within the Firm's framework and unspoken culture any longer. I became determined that I would not get to the end of my career and wonder, *Why didn't the guy behind blue eyes ever show up? Would I have been more productive if I left Big Law? Would I have reached a new level of excellence if I left the Firm?* It became clear that I would not face Jesus and have him ask me why I did not live the life that he created for me.

One day, in the middle of the Atlantic, we had an evacuation drill just in case we were attacked by pirates—Captain Phillips style. During the drill, I was told I did not need to participate in the exercise. *Hmmm.* So, I continued my solitary way of life on the bet that the container ship would make it to Italy with our current captain and crew intact.

How Does One Get a Fish Hook
Out of One's Mouth?

One morning Nicholas asked whether it was difficult to leave work. I explained how projects and issues were on my mind, and I hoped the associates were taking care of business. For the most part, I told him I was in the process of unplugging from the Firm. I was sure he did not believe me.

I continued to shift my thoughts towards living a life off the grid—Jason Bourne style. By unplugging to the extent I had for the last month, I realized how steep and fast the Big Law treadmill actually was. This realization was leading me to the possibility that I would not return to Big Law and instead take up residence somewhere else. Stepping outside the world of Big Law and reflecting on how hard I work was driving me away from all that I worked so hard to achieve.

I asked Nicholas if he found retirement challenging, and he responded, "Oh no. I have plenty of things to keep me busy." He spoke of a few things he missed and certain things that he was grateful not having to deal with any longer, such as internal school meetings and parent/teacher conferences. I mentioned that when it is time for a law partner to transition out of his or her job, it is something akin to taking a fish hook out of his or her mouth. One can hold on tight with a clenched jaw and have it hurt like hell, or one can relax and have it slip out with little blood spilled. I also pointed out that the fish (and the partners) who struggle often end up dead sooner than those fish (and partners) who relax and are set free to live another day.

My First Walkabout

After more than halfway across the Atlantic, I grabbed my rosary and asked Nicholas to take a walk with me "outside." This was my first time walking outside while the container ship was actually moving. It was my form of a "walkabout."

Walking around the ship was not a simple act of opening a door and just walking. There was a process to follow that red line. I first needed to clear it with the bridge, wear a reflective jacket and for insurance purposes, put on a hard helmet (as if that would protect me if a container fell on top of me). Nonetheless, I stepped outside with Nicholas close by without a care in the world (except fear of tripping and falling overboard.

My first walkabout.

And my curiosity did not come close to negating this fear).

It felt good to get outside and finally walk somewhere other than to the dining hall. Once outside, I stayed vigilant to walking that red line. To say I walked with a purpose is an understatement. But once I navigated my way to the bow, I relaxed and began breathing normally again. I even smiled while leaning against the anchor. I enjoyed watching the water pass by. The sea was so calm. I could have stayed for hours soaking up the sun. I felt nothing but peace.

A REFLECTIVE MOMENT: While sitting in the sun and watching the Atlantic Ocean go by, I decided I needed to experience life from a different dimension. I had never been a person to live a lifestyle of keeping up with the Joneses or keeping up with society as society thought one should, but I was good at appearing as if I did. After all, I, like all my other 300 closest friends, was a partner pinned to a partnership contract. I did the marriage, three kids, house, a beach house, an occasional theater appearance and the like, but in my heart that appearance stuff was not me. It was not my essence. I genuinely love my family, and I will always be there for them, but the other material stuff felt more like a coat/shield/mask covering my true self—covering my true adventurous self. Now all of this might sound like some psycho-babble BS, but I have always been intrigued by out-of-the-box ideas (like taking a container ship). I firmly believe that all progress in life is made outside the proverbial box of conventional life, and while sitting outside on the deck of a container ship in the middle of the Atlantic Ocean, I came to recognize it was time to get on with living the life I was meant to live. To be the man that God created me to be. As each day passed, my experiment of unplugging from the Firm machine was leading me to an extraordinary course correction in my life.

If we are going to do anything significant with life, we sometimes have to move away from it—beyond the usual measurements. We must occasionally follow visions and dreams.

—Fr. Bede Jarrett

May 18—Mount St. Helen's Day

My BlackBerry exploded with vibration late one night as the container ship approached the Straits of Gibraltar. I knew I was back in AT&T range and needed to deal with two weeks' worth of unanswered emails. While lying in bed, I was not looking forward to scrolling through them all; so instead, I emailed my kids. It was good to catch-up with them and let them know I was doing well *and was still alive.*

On my last full day in the Atlantic, the ocean was smooth, and the sun was shining brightly. This made for a picturesque moment as we slipped by the "Rock" and into the Mediterranean Sea. However, work occupied my mind as I dreaded responding to two weeks' of emails. I felt as if I had done an admirable job of unplugging from Big Law. My unplugging experience seemed to work. I could appreciate how awesome the Firm had been to me. It allowed me to send all three kids to college, paid for a beautiful house and allowed me to raise a nice family, but I still had this strong pull inside of me that I had run my course with the Firm and needed some sort of shift in behavior. I began to think that a monastic life was a preferable way to spending my remaining years rather than returning to the 47th floor and drafting retirement plans.

You won't kill yourself by doing it; you will kill yourself by not doing it.

—Unknown

When I turned 50, I read Jonathan Franzen's book, *Freedom*. While reading this book, I came to the conclusion that people cannot handle their freedom. They stay locked in doing life, staying at a mediocre job, at best, and never really experiencing what life has to offer. Taking the Adventure was a first step in becoming free from a programmed life. This freedom, however, was not easy to create nor at times was it a secure and comfy feeling. Writing a manuscript and delivering it to the managing partner while suspecting that he believed I had lost my mind was a difficult conversation. Explaining to him that I was willing to quit to travel the world was not exactly a bed of roses, emotionally speaking.

But in creating this Adventure and unplugging from Big Law my soul awakened to something unfamiliar and profound. I began to realize how locked and trapped I felt when I was at work. I was not free and I had to do something. Big Law creates an illusion that Big Law is "it" in your working life (and any other job means you are not living up to your potential). But one is not free if their existence is tied to billing an incredible amount of hours. My journey of unplugging from the Big Law machine and experiencing freedom in a different way led me to the brink of abandoning Big Law.

While the container ship hugged the northern coast of Africa, I realized I could make an exit from Big Law with grace. For the first time, I had no fear of not returning to Big Law. Work would always exist, and I could always have work back if and when I decided to re-enter Big Law. Freedom was a beautiful thing.

Game On

As the container ship entered the Straits of Gibraltar in the early evening, lots of other container ships' lights could be seen from the G deck. I stared out with a beer in hand and watched the sun fall into the water. It was a beautiful sunset. The anticipation of land plus being told that we had an overnight in port was all very exciting. The Ukrainian officers gave me some shore tips on where to eat and otherwise just hang out. They were also very excited for a shore leave. I guess they wanted to have a little R&R to celebrate another Atlantic crossing.

After we docked in Algeciras, Spain, for the night, I headed into

town for a little exploration and a proper dinner. I was looking forward
to eating at a restaurant, ordering off a menu and having food that did
not have to be defrosted and was served by a waiter. But most of all I
was welcoming a break from chicken noodle soup. As I was heading
back to the ship after a delicious dinner of fresh fish and vegetables,
I ran into the Ukrainians. They were sitting at an outdoor café sipping
vodka. I joined them, and we had some good laughs about being a
sailor. They were clearly eyeing some local ladies, but the vodka was
preventing the hook-up they desired. It was a scene where a sober
52-year-old man was watching young drunk guys who didn't speak
Spanish try and wow some local birds. The lines they were using in
broken English were hilarious, and the young ladies had no idea what
they were saying. It was fun to watch some 30-year-olds try.

You can check-out anytime you like, but you can never leave.
—The Eagles, *Hotel California* (aka going on a two-week vacation
                            and trying to unplug from the Firm)

Here is what I realized while sitting in the Spanish port: I care
about my family. I care about my clients. I care about my Firm, and I
care about my work. Yes, I do love ERISA work. I don't understand
why more people don't practice this type of law, and I can't imagine
practicing any other type. Most of all, I could not imagine working
anywhere else. But here I was going through a transition phase. I
knew that Big Law, in general, was hard on many different levels. It is
difficult to (a) obtain and retain clients, (b) make sure associates are
treating clients the proper way and (c) complete all the administrative
work that goes along with clients in Big Law (such as billings and timely
collections). On top of all this, one had to deal with the egos of the
true rainmakers, partners who think they are rainmakers, and of course,
the former rainmakers who believe they are still making it rain. This
reality show was snowballing into a decision to move away from Big Law.

In fact, while being mesmerized by the loading and unloading
of containers, I concluded that it was time to cowboy-up and do
something significant with my life. I was ready to move beyond Firm

politics, measurements (who gets paid more, who gets a bonus, who works the most hours, etc.) and to distinguish myself as a modern day adventurer. If not now, when? I didn't want to regret not doing something extraordinary when I was too old to make a course correction. I needed to focus on what was next in my life.

Spectacular Sunrise Over the Rock

As we left Algeciras, the sunrise over the Rock of Gibraltar was simply remarkable. Sitting on the G deck, sipping on a cup of coffee, taking in the beautiful early morning sun that shined on the Rock, watching the calm sea and heavenly blue sky made for a picturesque, relaxing moment. That same morning while exercising, I ran into the ship's electrician and (a) I was glad to see that he made it in from the wild night and (b) we both had some laughs about our shore leave.

Leaving the Atlantic Ocean.

As the ship hugged the coast of North Africa heading east toward Malta, our next port, I was sitting out on the G deck playing my guitar and reflecting on being at a gorgeous outdoor café with a cup of coffee and not thinking about, reading nor responding to any of the work calls or emails from the prior two weeks. I had no intention of living a monastic life, but I wondered if life would be fulfilling if I just read, wrote, biked, swam, ran and traveled for the next 25 years. The clearer the possibility of not returning to Big Law became, the more excited I became about starting down a different path. A path of conscious choice. Excitement. Exploration. Adventure.

Sailing in the Mediterranean focused my attention that my unplugging experiment via a container ship was coming to an end. Nicholas and I still had some beers left. We began to have pre-dinner drinks as well as a nightcap while watching the sun do its thing. I also began to play more guitar with Nesto, the head chef. We would meet up around 8:30 p.m. and play and sing to old classic songs from Cat Stevens and the Beatles. Nesto was a great guitarist and could also carry a tune. In my last week on the container ship, we spent some late nights jamming in the kitchen next to the stove. My leftover bottle of wine from dinner made our guitar picking even that much better. These nights were a blast. Just he and I in an empty kitchen thinking we were modern day rock stars.

Breakfast with Nicholas

After a stormy night (a full moon the cause?) on our way to Italy, Nicholas shared a book he wrote about freighters. It was fascinating. He had a love for the history of freighters, and I enjoyed learning about them. We also spoke more about freighter travel and its slow pace compared to an airplane and even a cruise ship. I explained how some people I told about my freighter trip and the solitude I would experience really understood it and envied me but at the same time could never see themselves doing this sort of trip. I explained how I really hoped my Adventure would broaden people's perspective on their ability to take a break and do something similar. "I pity those who don't understand what you are doing," was Nicholas' remark. I happen to agree.

Cabin Fever

Disguising our insignificance by the dignity of hurry.
                            —Samuel Johnson, *The Rambler* No. 142

In the days leading up to my departure from the container ship, I experienced a bit of cabin fever. Twenty-nine days was enough for a maiden voyage. Plus, I received an email from the Cape Town running club and was invited on some runs, including a half marathon. This jump started my thoughts and excitement for the post-freighter part of my Adventure.

I also read more of *The Rambler*. I found Samuel Johnson's 1750s writings very relevant to Big Law. For example, he dedicated an entire issue about disguising one's insignificance. His writing made me think of how lawyers in Big Law often disguise their insignificance by appearing to be in a hurry. There is a perception we need to create that next billable hour—all in what now appears to me as a way to disguise our insignificance. A lawyer in Big Law who is not in a hurry is attributed the deadly perception that he/she has no work. We are all taught that prospective clients want to always hire the busy lawyers, so we all act busy even when we have a break in work for 24 hours. A crazy way to live life—disguising one's insignificance by the dignity of hurry. We never slow down even when work is slow.

The view of northern Africa from the G deck was truly amazing. There was a beauty to the miles of uninhabited beach with a backdrop of rocky mountains. Much of the African coastline was isolated and rugged; it created a pull within me to jump overboard and swim to shore. There were also many small uninhabited islands along the way which would appear out of nowhere. These islands had a beauty I had never seen before. I pondered what life on a deserted island would be like. Maybe it would be similar to the TV series *Lost* and a great adventure would unfold. I was certain my BlackBerry would not work.

But as we moved more and more into the Mediterranean, the captain was forced to maneuver among the many other container ships on their way to Europe. Watching other container ships became mesmerizing. With the help of Nicholas, I began to notice the different types of container ships. Nicholas could distinguish between the container ships that carried cars, raw materials as well as crap like we had. Hours would fly by as I (and sometimes Nicholas) would stare out over the sea and watch the world just pass by.

Livorno, Italy—*Live Well*

Nicholas left the ship when we stopped in Livorno, Italy. It was sad to see a good friend leave. I will forever remember him and our conversations, especially those we had while having pre-dinner beers on the G deck. He taught me a lot about travel and the pure joy of traveling by means other than an airplane. The more I got to know Nicholas the more I thought it would have been a joy to have him as a teacher (even if I would not have received an A in his class). "Live well" were my last words to him as he carefully walked down the gangway.

CHAPTER SEVEN

INTRODUCE THOUGHT BACK INTO YOUR LIFE

Waking Up on Land

My first day on land was awesome. I disembarked the container ship in Genoa and hopped a train to swanky Portofino. After I checked into a random (quaint and excessively expensive) hotel and had a great talk with the proprietor, I went for an incredible run from Portofino to San Fruttuoso. I ran along a path that gripped to cliffs 100 meters above the sea. The views were amazing.

The village of San Fruttuoso is known for the Christ of the Abyss. It has a submerged bronze statue of Jesus Christ that was placed in the water in 1954 at approximately 60 feet deep and stands nine feet tall. The statue was placed near the spot where Dario Gonzatti, the first Italian to use scuba gear, died in 1947. It depicts Christ with his head and hands raised towards the sky offering a blessing of peace.

As adventurous as I am, I was not inspired to dive in and seek out the statue. I simply took up a place on the beach and people watched with a bottle of water in hand. This quaint little village was a beautiful

off-the-typical-tourist-path village with stunning sights. It was the first
of many off-the-beaten-path spots I would discover on my Adventure.

Portofino was spectacular—very high end and right on the water.
Boats, or more appropriately said, yachts, were literally jammed in the
small port area with their owners sipping wine and eating fancy hors
d'oeuvres. Sitting outside overlooking these yachts with a nice glass
of wine was relaxing. Watching the rich mingle on their million dollar
yachts and people walking around under a sky full of stars was hard
to beat. I was invited aboard one enormous yacht for a glass of wine
by a very nice and adventurous couple who were in their early 60s.
This couple obviously had more than enough cash to not only own
a yacht but to employ a captain and crew as well! As they inquired
about my Adventure, I sensed they had regrets about not doing the
adventure thing earlier in life.

My first day back on land.

As I settled into my hotel room for my first night without sailors
down the hall, I thought about Samuel Johnson and his observation
of when one takes a step back and looks at life, it could drive one into
a monastery. I worked extremely hard and I was very dedicated to the
Firm and my clients, but I felt trapped and anything but free with my
work life. I was ready to flee. Thinking back on my 25-plus years at
the Firm and what I was feeling in that moment, never returning to

Big Law was the next logical step—but I knew taking up a monastic lifestyle was not in the cards for me at all.

So at the very least, ask yourself this hypothetical question today, 'If I had no fear, if I imagine that failure is not an option, what would I do and when would I do it?' The answer, I suspect, would be 'now.'
—Alastair Humphreys, Blogger

A Shave and the Beach

Having ignored shaving while with a bunch of sailors, I decided it was time to clean up. I found the sole barber in the entire village and got a haircut and shave—Italian style. Hot towels and a shave with a straight razor were the perfect way to start a day. I then went on a nine-mile run on the beach followed by some bread, cheese and pesto from the local market. What a beautiful morning.

I had been emailing my mom and talking with her more often than ever through an app called Viber (similar to Skype). I really came to love her more and more as an incredible person and terrific mom. She is devoted to her children and grandchildren and is such a great example for me to follow. She was very supportive of my Adventure, and it felt great to have her in my corner. My awareness of her love for me was the biggest eye opener on my Adventure.

On the Move to Milano

I am sitting at the railway station with a ticket for my destination...
—Simon & Garfunkel, "Homeward Bound"

I was off to Milan for two nights and was looking forward to being in a large city. On the train, I sat next to a person who only spoke Italian, and it was so much fun to practice my Italian. Normally, I would have just sat quietly next to the guy minding my own business. I have always felt it was safer to keep my mouth shut and not be expressive, just hang out, don't make waves and people will come to the conclusion that Mark is just a nice guy. Most people just don't know who I am and what makes me tick. That is why many people were shocked when they heard I was taking an Adventure. I seem to surprise people by the things I do. And I didn't want to do that anymore. I want people to say, "Mark is getting the most out of life and is an adventurous soul." Sure, I may be nonconventional by Big Law standards, but I am conventional by my own standards.

On the train, I committed to no longer simply sit back and watch the days go by. I was now committed to joining the game of life as an active and vocal participant. This new commitment made me think of Katy Perry's song *Roar* and its lyrics:

> I used to bite my tongue and hold my breath
> Scared to rock the boat and make a mess
> So I sat quietly, agreed politely
> I guess that I forgot I had a choice...

What hit me about this song was how much I bit my tongue with internal work issues. I never spoke up thinking I was keeping the peace and doing the right thing, Firm wise. You could say that I took Aaron Burr's advice to Alexander Hamilton in the "talk less and smile more" approach to life. I was the good law partner that no one had to worry about. I was predictable and dependable. I was at work early and stayed late. Clients could reach me 24/7, and I delivered a solu-

tion to their every issue. I never let on to my frustrations. In that Katy Perry moment, I committed to no longer holding back and waiting for the perfect time to speak up in all aspects of my life. I had earned the right to speak up in any and all situations. I became committed to not sit quietly while others determined my path forward. So, while sitting next to this guy, I not only broke out with some below average Italian, I also got my guitar out and jammed

Jamming on a train to Milan.

to "This Old Man." I was not sure what made him laugh louder, my Italian or my guitar skills.

A Life Fully Lived—the Goal

Well, I showed up at my beyond fancy and very high priced Milan hotel completely underdressed in filthy, smelly trekking pants and boots. I was actually surprised they allowed me to register. I was now facing a different problem. I had no pants other than my reeking trekking ones nor any other shoes to wear for the next three days. After taking a long, hot shower in a fancy bathroom, I headed out to find clothes. I found a store I had never heard before called *Zegna* right off the bat, and I bought some unreasonably priced shoes, a pair of pants and a shirt. I'm sure the nice lady who helped me wanted me out of the store as quickly as possible, and I'm positive they were not pleased with me leaving behind my smelly clothes, but I was.

Elevate Your Brand

I could not leave the fashion capital of the world without some Gucci shopping—yes, even I had to get some shopping done. Following lunch on my last day in Milan, I was off to the Gucci store in my snappy looking Zegna clothes. I settled on a severely overpriced traditional Gucci wallet. It was a fun experience, and for the first time in my life, I actually enjoyed shopping, even if I will never be mistaken for a fashionista.

CHAPTER EIGHT

_____

I AM NEVER RETURNING

It is easier to stay out than to get out.

—Mark Twain

I boarded the container ship with a determination to unplug and distance myself from Big Law for four months, seeking a simple, and well needed, pause in life. I knew nothing other than the Firm and Big Law, and I needed a break from the daily grind. As I journeyed down the road of unplugging, I went through many different emotions, and while sitting on the plane from Milan to Cape Town, I realized in that exact moment that I was professionally complete with my Big Law career. I felt I had no unfinished business, and I was NOT going back to Big Law. I had expanded an already excellent ERISA practice and knew the team back on the 47th floor would be fine. The clients would also be fine. I knew that leaving Big Law was not a mistake; professional "failure" was not a possibility for me. I had a "been there, done that" state of mind going on. I never intended to move in this new direction back in January 2013. However, I now wanted to discover what life was outside of a suit and tie, sitting behind a desk with an ear phone and a stack of pension plans to review. It was clear that a monastic lifestyle was not the road to travel, but my experiment of unplugging produced a radically different outcome. One that I was not expecting.

I was determined to live life from a new dimension. A life based on adventure and not a life based on billable hours producing a slow death to my soul. Repeating the past for the next 13 or more years was just unacceptable to me. My past was way too present in my daily existence, and I wanted out. Mark Twain summed it up by saying that it is easier to stay out [of Big Law] than to get out [at least on my terms].

I was very in tune with my newfound realization of being done with Big Law. I was living on this incredibly fast treadmill, at such a steep pitch, and I was stepping aside. Although I have described Big Law as a fast treadmill over the years, I had never actually experienced stepping off the treadmill until that point in time. Working out three to five hours per day, reading and writing *plus* a nap here and there had shown me a new way to live life. A way that life should be lived. A way I wanted *my* life to be lived. My decision had nothing to do with how Big Law operates. I was grateful for what Big Law had provided me, not only financially, but the growth I experienced as a lawyer, but more importantly, as a person. I simply wanted, and became committed, to elevating my life to the next level. I became committed to pursuing a new way of life. This monumental decision not to return created a relief throughout my body, even more relief than what I experienced when I descended in that elevator on my last day of work back in April.

And then there is the most dangerous risk of all—the risk of spending your life not doing what you want on the bet you can buy yourself the freedom to do it later.
—Randy Komisar, *The Monk and the Riddle: The Education of a Silicon Valley Entrepreneur*

While getting settled into my overnight flight from Milan to Cape Town, South Africa (SA), I let my mind wander to all the things I would like to experience before transcending into Heaven. The mental freedom from Big Law that I was experiencing had me wanting to become more conscious of my life choices going forward. I was no longer set on autopilot mode of working at the Firm for 13 more years. I imagined how good life would be if every decision I made reflected exactly what I wanted to do, even if the decision was a conscious spur of the moment decision. Age 65 used to seem a long way off, but it was less than 13 years away. It was time to cowboy-up and become more aware of my life.

Cape Town, known as South Africa's "Mother City," is a marvelous place to visit. Legend has it that in the 1930s a local Cape Town newspaper claimed that Cape Town was the only city in South Africa that could justly call itself a metropolis (taken from the Greek derivative of meter/metros meaning mother and polis meaning city). From this, the nickname Mother City was born.

As the plane was landing, I caught a glimpse of Table Mountain. It was the jewel of Cape Town, the number one tourist destination and a sight to see. It was just as stark and beautiful as Mount Rainier. On clear days, Table Mountain stood out looking all over Cape Town just as Mount Rainier overlooks Seattle, and similar to Seattle, clear days were rare when I was in Cape Town.

A REFLECTIVE MOMENT: Exploration should be experienced by all lawyers. Exploration will lead curious, happy and creative lawyers to a place where they can discover, have a new understanding and find opportunities for growth that others will seek.

That first night in SA, I was excited to receive an email from Nicholas. His introduction to Samuel Johnson (and *The Rambler*) had a significant impact on me and my Adventure. One essay about taking time off from one's high stature to look at life changed the entire dynamic of my Adventure. I began my Gap Period with a single memo indicating I was taking time off from work. I had no idea that I would be transitioning into leaving Big Law and into walking down a road never before traveled.

Table Mountain

My first full day in Cape Town began with a climb of Table Mountain. The hotel cautioned me not to go it alone. They were concerned I would run into some undesirables on the trail and all that goes along with that. But I did it anyway, and it was all good (the few locals I met on the trail left me alone). The climb was much more difficult than I expected. Seventy percent of the trail was very manageable, but the other thirty percent was challenging. Some parts required me to be on all fours. It took over four hours to climb up, and my heart was definitely racing. Once I reached the top, the views were unbelievably spectacular. The entire coastline was right before my eyes. The ocean, rugged coastline and the crashing waves could be seen for miles on both sides of Cape Town. There was nothing but sunshine in the sky. Sitting on a rock taking in this sight was a great way to catch my breath from the trek up the mountain. As for the way down the mountain, I opted for the five-minute tram ride.

Table Mountain.

Later that night, I met up with a Cape Town running club. But before the run, I replaced my only pair of smelly running shoes and shorts. A smelly foreigner had no chance to meet some interesting locals.

We met along the shore and went for a three-mile out and back. Everyone in the group was super nice. They even had a slow group they referred to as "penguins" (and no, I did not run with this group). After the run, a group of ten of us went to grab some beers. Hanging with the locals and hearing about the local races, such as Comrades, had me excited about a return trip. Following our beers, I bummed a ride back to the hotel. One cannot go wrong hanging with runners—they're always a cool bunch.

While staying in Cape Town, I found a local Bikram yoga studio. At my first class, the instructor stated the class was to be devoted to focusing on thoughts that transpire between the inhale and exhale of a breath. Between that millisecond of inhaling and exhaling many thoughts occupied my mind, from total peace and relaxation to frustration and anger. It was all very mindful to be aware of thoughts for 90 minutes in a hot and humid yoga room.

Insanity: doing the same thing over and over again and expecting different results.

—Albert Einstein (attributed)

A REFLECTIVE MOMENT: "Expectations" are simply seeds of resentment. Postponing exploration and adventure with the expectation that it will happen in the future will result in resentment when one is unable to actualize it. The time is now to become the person God created you to be.

A Cold and Rainy Day in the Cape

I woke very early one rainy morning and went for a long run. The cold rain slapped my face with every step I made. Listening to the sound of the water crashing against the dark rocky shore as I ran along the endless coastline made for a peaceful and calming run. With every breath I took, the smell of the ocean was soothing. The solitude reminded me of my days back on the container ship, and I was really missing them, the crew and Nicholas too.

Prior to leaving Houston, I scheduled a client video conference call for when I was in Cape Town. I spent a full day preparing for this video call, and all the while I questioned, *Why on God's green earth did I do this? I should have had an associate take care of the "emergency."* The thoughts and feelings I was experiencing about taking this call were another indication of why I needed to move beyond Big Law and its illusions of a glamorous lifestyle.

While visiting a foreign office was intriguing, my excitement of feeling alive in this world crashed when I added the fragment of work into the mix of things. What was even more disappointing and difficult to tolerate was dealing with lawyers on the other side of a transaction and their big egos, who were more concerned with appearing *right* than solving the issue at hand. And yes, I know it's surprising that *those* lawyers exist in Big Law. Dealing with those types was more than I could take at that point in my work life. Some lawyers just cannot help from being self-centered jerks, and I was tired of pounding my head against the proverbial wall and hoping things would be different.

That afternoon I slipped into autopilot work mode, and I really did not like who I became. I was hooked, once again, into a robotic, mechanical conveyor of spot on legal advice. My true essence was completely shut down. The extreme contrast I experienced that particular afternoon of my way of *being* was self-evident, and it made me realize why I needed to unplug and move on. I had evolved. The pettiness and insecurities of others were not the distinguished behaviors I wanted to be a part of any longer. As I sat in the conference room following the call, slouched in a chair with a cold cup of coffee in hand staring at a blank video screen, I was amazed that in one short month I had admirably unplugged from the daily existence of Big Law.

After a full day of work, I needed to refocus on why I was here— my Adventure. So I headed to the waterfront section of town for a pre-dinner walk. It was good to get out and watch couples and families walking around on such a beautiful night. I struck up conversations with tourists from all over the world, and I noticed that many people I met either felt sorry for me for traveling solo or envied it, but in both cases, they were more than willing to buy me drinks.

One night I decided to try the tapas at the hotel's famed Whiskey Bar. While minding my own business and enjoying some delicious tapas, I could not ignore the chatter of a group of women in their 30s and an overweight 55-year-old bald businessman in town via a luxurious yacht docked right outside. The guy had the cash and the bar tab going (in a huge way). He was buying the group drinks and expensive champagne. I couldn't help but find it interesting, and amusing, to watch and listen to their loud conversations. As I struck up a chat with one of the women, he butted in swiftly thinking I was hitting on one of his "gals." As the three of us talked, he lightened up and invited me into his inner circle of fun. I was more than happy to drink his expensive champagne and hang with his entourage. It turned out that he had worked with my Firm in the past on a corporate transaction—small world.

As the night progressed, a weird thing happened. He decided to wash the feet of one of the ladies, who had a nice pair of leather boots on, with champagne. The woman was hesitant, but he prevailed and proceeded to wash her feet with the champagne. Now this may have been one of those events that you needed to be there, but what started out looking like a funny act by a drunk dude, turned into a complete mess with champagne everywhere and a not so happy lady. I felt bad for her and the cleaners. As the bar announced its last call, the group decided to hit some local clubs. But because all decisions that involve alcohol and are made after 2 a.m. are bad decisions, I decided to pass on this one and let the fat, bald guy have his fun. I'm positive that all he got that night was a very large bill.

Better weight than wisdom a traveler cannot carry.

—Viking Proverb

A REFLECTIVE MOMENT: Another unspoken code of Big Law is that lawyers seem to look and act in a uniform manner. Distinguished, positive behavior seldom transpires, but instead, we all become a blended sort. An adventure will awaken a soul from a deeply frozen existence of repetitive behavior. There are real alternatives to an hour-by-hour daily existence in life.

I made it to a second Bikram yoga class. The instructor began the class with a saying, "Life is intense, but one gets to choose how one handles the intensity." And the class *was* intense but AWESOME. This also made me think of my career. Big Law *is* intense. We are paid handsomely, but it is nonetheless intense. A break from work is encouraged as long as it does not last more than a week (at most, if you're lucky). While on vacation one is expected to carry a BlackBerry/ cell phone with him/her at all times and expected to check and return emails and calls daily. That is just the state of Big Law. One cannot escape no matter how far one travels nor how fancy the resort where one stays. Demanding clients, real or imagined, are always prevalent in a Big Law lawyer's mindset. One cannot simply unplug and disconnect from this lifestyle. By stepping off the Big Law treadmill and all of its steepness, intensity and speed and standing completely still in *tree pose* on a sweaty yoga mat, I felt completely satisfied that my decision to leave Big Law was correct. I could not continue repeating the intensity of the past. I was unplugged and it felt great. *Namaste* I said to myself as I left the hot and humid yoga room.

As the days passed, I was becoming more and more present of "being" in this world. Going to the office and "doing" the work thing just did not fuel me anymore. It no longer was an adrenaline hit. I achieved all the professional accolades I could imagine, and spending the next 10 to 15 years doing repetitive work was a mountain not worth climbing (and I love climbing mountains). One afternoon, while sitting on a random bench overlooking the ocean, I became very excited to begin a walk into the unknown of my life.

Nobody ever died of discomfort, yet living in the name of comfort has killed more ideas, more opportunities, more actions, and more growth than everything else combined. Comfort Kills!

—T. Harv Eker

Father's Day

I began my nearly three-week road trip up the Garden Route and the Wild Coast to Durban. My first stop was a small beach town, St. James, where I was the only guest at a quaint hotel. The hotel had a fire going just for me (or so I told myself) to warm-up on a cold night. Sitting on a couch with a glass of red wine with a roaring fire made for a memorable 2013 Father's Day. The only thing that could have made the day more complete was if my three children were with me.

St. James had the reputation of being a low-key "surfer town" and a great place to explore. So, on my first morning I located a coffee house right on the beach and watched the surfers do their thing. Everyone seemed to be more concerned about having a hot cup of coffee and catching big waves than rushing off to work. The "no rush" vibe was tranquilizing.

St. James.

I felt life was getting better by the moment. Unplugging from Big Law made me realize how liberating life can really be. Choosing a new path and not being bound by a time card back on the 47th floor was the way I wanted to live life.

Most of us have two lives. The life we live, and the unlived life within us. Between the two stands Resistance.
—Steven Pressfield, *The War of Art*

Surfing South African Style

What could be better than waking up on my last morning in St. James to the sound of a train and the crashing of waves. I couldn't help but head out for a run on the beach. While running, I noticed a group of surfers who seemed to be experiencing that magical feeling of flying, of being one with the waves. It had me thinking of the differences between doing, being and experiencing. I wanted to move away from just doing things in life and move towards really *experiencing* life. I had become a master of the "do" in the work world, and it no longer brought me any meaning other than an accomplishment to be listed on my résumé. I could *do* pension plans and 401(k) plans really well, but this was no longer fulfilling. I felt I had moved beyond simply being in this world as well. For me, to "be" is similar to being in the moment, like sitting on a yoga mat meditating on life (the goal of every yoga teacher), and I am just too active to simply be in this world. I wanted to transform myself and have maximum experiences. I wanted to have that magical feeling like a surfer on a perfect wave and become one with all that life has to offer.

The world is a book and those who do not travel read only one page.
—St. Augustine of Hippo

I was very excited to visit a wine region in South Africa that rivaled Napa. The wine region is known as Stellenbosch. As I was driving, I first stopped at the Cape of Good Hope. The drive along the ocean was majestic. Watching the violent waves crashing against a rugged shoreline was a sight to see. However, the jagged mountains, the steepness and sharp angles of each cliff, did not lure me into wanting to climb. I arrived in Stellenbosch just after dusk, which made finding my hotel a serious challenge.

Great things are done when men and mountains meet.
—William Blake

I signed up for a wine tour that would make six different winery stops. The upside to this was that you could get dropped back in town at any point during the tour. The office disclosed that very few tourists actually make *all* six stops. I smiled and mentally accepted a new challenge—I intended to be a part of the few that made *all* six stops. *Game on!*

The wine at the first stop was delicious. I casually spoke with the server about local restaurants, and he not only gave me the name of an authentic Afrikaans restaurant located near my hotel, but even made my reservation. As expected, I purchased a bottle of Pinotage, a true South African red. After some more drinking at the second and third wineries, I realized I wasn't going to make all six stops. I asked to be dropped off after the third stop. I thanked the local tourist office for a phenomenal wine tour, at least for three stops, as I walked back to my hotel.

A wine tour stop.

Leaving Stellenbosch

I was not sure what I ate at my Afrikaans dinner, but it had some type of meat as the main dish and it was delicious. I sat next to a couple from Cape Town (based on the silly and flirtatious conversations and lack of wedding rings, it appeared to be a one-night stand for them), and we had some good laughs about traveling, wine and talking with strangers. As I was leaving, they invited me to Cape Town to meet some of their single friends. Although tempting, I told them I was headed north up the Wild Coast, which they promised would be a beautiful drive.

After dinner, I went to the hotel lounge area, had another glass of wine, sat by a comforting fire and struck up a conversation with a woman who was also enjoying the fire. She was in town presenting a paper at the local university on how South Africa, as a nation, is co-dependent on the government to provide assistance to its people. She was really keyed up on the topic. After two glasses of wine, her excitement was overwhelming. Trying to change a nation was just not my cup of tea at this stage in my life.

A REFLECTIVE MOMENT: Adult life has many stages, like seasons in a year. School, marriage, kids and work. And it is important to accept each change in season. This includes embracing a change in one's career path. A future beyond Big Law should be about experiencing things, places and people, not out of personal growth (because I detest phrases like that), but because we all have inquisitive souls. I intend to explore the world for the simple purpose of exploring the next seasons of life. I intend to live like I am watching a movie on life that never ends and I am the star.

Plettenberg Bay

I left Stellenbosch thanking God my mission in life was not to change a nation, but rather, to navigate a beautiful drive to Plettenberg Bay (Plett to the locals). I arrived early morning and found a coffee shop overlooking a peaceful, picturesque white beach and sat to watch the spectacular sunrise over the ocean while sipping on a hot cup of coffee. A couple next to me asked about my rental car, and this led to a great conversation about the slow pace of life one can live in Plett. It turned out that the guy previously worked and lived in Dallas. They gave me the low down on Plett and places to hang out at night. They mentioned that the coffee shop turned into quite the restaurant in the evenings and as I looked around, it did have that hangover type of energy.

I checked out the coffee bar that evening, and it was a happening place. Lots of locals relaxing on the large deck enjoying a beautiful sunset with cold beers in hand listening to some *Searching for Sugarman* music. Everyone was friendly. Speaking with people about life outside of a cubicle working 40-plus hours a week makes for fun conversations. Several people thought I was crazy for taking such a trip solo. However, I sensed they envied my journey. This became a common experience as the Adventure unfolded.

On my last day in Plett, I went on an amazing three-hour late afternoon hike alongside the cliffs of the ocean. The views were spectacular, as I could see sailboats and whales enjoying a beautiful sunny day. When I returned to the hotel, a wedding celebration of a beautiful couple in their early 50s was taking place. Nearly 50 people attended, and they were all incredibly welcoming as they handed me a glass of wine. I felt like Vince Vaughn and Owen Wilson in the *Wedding Crashers*. There was lots of food, fresh fish, meat and lots of sweets, and let's not forget plenty of delicious wine. I stayed to the bitter end (since I had no place else to go) with a few of the single members of the wedding party. I don't recall what we talked about, but I sure had a lot of fun.

Jeffrey's Bay

My next stop was Jeffrey's Bay, a well-known surfer town. After finding a hotel, I stopped by a surf store and got the low down on the local surfer hangout spots. There is something about surfers and my ability to connect with them. They remind me of mountain guides in the sense that I could sit and talk with them for hours.

A REFLECTIVE MOMENT: In Big Law, vacation is not always taken. Some say this is another unspoken code of Big Law behavior. Whether the reason is fear of (a) asking one's supervisor, (b) losing a prized assignment or (c) disappointing a client, lawyers seldom take breaks. This is evident by the massive amounts of carried over and unused vacation days accumulated by the end of a career. And because unused vacation days are not paid out, it highlights how much work is valued over vacations with family. Burnout, overwork and the buildup of frustration would be minimized if breaks were not only encouraged, but required to be taken.

Located on a sandy beach was a super cool restaurant that served only fresh seafood caught that day called The Kitchen. While I was having dinner there, a spectacularly bright and giant moon was shining above me. It was the day following a supermoon, and the moon was so close that it seemed as though you could touch it. As the diners left, the kitchen staff invited me to hang with them while they cleaned up. Hanging with restaurant staff post-closing had sure become my staple of friends.

The next morning I woke around 5:30 a.m. thinking, *What the hell am I doing?* I thought going on a crazy adventure, unplugging from Big Law and deciding never to return were each terrible decisions, and put all together, completely insane. Talk about getting up on the wrong side of the bed!

I went to the lounge to check out my route to Port St. Johns, my next stop. I also read the lyrics to a couple of Mumford & Sons songs I had downloaded. I really came to enjoy their music. Some of their lyrics hit deep within my core, like the lyrics to "Awake My Soul." Focusing on waking my soul from 25-plus years of the hallows of Big Law and how I had been "doing" life as a lawyer on the 47th floor was enough to overcome my *what the hell am I doing* mood.

With Pleasure

Throughout SA, when you thanked the wait staff, they sincerely responded, "With pleasure." It was a genuinely simple comment that made a huge impression on the purchasing experience. It really made me want to buy more. If lawyers could adopt the *with pleasure* attitude toward clients, they will buy more legal services.

A Trip Up the Wild Coast

On my nine-hour drive to the next hotel, I experienced a side of SA I was not expecting—negotiating traffic violations with police. Within a few hours into my drive, I was pulled over for speeding. I'm the type to mostly obey the speed limit, but this time I *was* speeding—along with many other cars—but I was the one who got busted. I was planning to plead my case to avoid a visit to the local station. Well, the officer made it very easy for me. His first words were, "Give me $120," and he would let me go. Since I was slightly scared, being in a foreign country, I gave him the cash and went on my way, cursing the SA police all the way.

A few hours later I was pulled over for "illegally" passing a car.

This time, there were many cars pulled over by the local police—all of them conveniently rentals. Now I was pissed. This was clearly a trap for tourists who were more concerned with driving on the left side of the highway than with passing lanes. As the officer approached my car, I needed to come up with a good excuse since I was all out of cash. I tried everything. Nothing seemed to work. After 30 minutes of trying to get out of this scam and becoming more frustrated by the minute, I held out my two hands and said, "Cuff me and bring me to the station." I was no longer in the mood to hand over cash I did not have, nor my watch, which they were eyeing (a cheap Timex). This created immediate panic on their side of the conversation. I'm sure they were questioning why this crazy American was asking to be taken to the station in cuffs. After some frantic Afrikaans between the two officers, they assured me they were not going to arrest me. They ended up letting me go and told me not to do what I did again. I drove off with the sole goal of not being pulled over *again* for the remainder of my time in SA

When I was not conversing with police, the scenery up the Wild Coast was amazing. It had a Texas Hill Country look and feel (rugged mountains with trees sparsed among the rocks) but with huge gorges and massive bridges. However, it was the goats, sheep, cows and even a pig, together with the massive potholes, that kept my eyes on the road.

All Is Good in Port St. Johns

I read about Port St. Johns in a guidebook and felt that it was a must-stop. The best that I could tell was that there were no hotels in this village, only backpacker lodges. The guidebooks discuss how people show up for a few days and end up never leaving. I now understood that phenomenon as I witnessed it with my own eyes.

As I sat outside my run-down backpacker lodge, where many guests were loitering about, the smell of pot was in full bloom. I had not stayed at a place like this since I was in college. I'm not quite sure how to describe this lodge—*was it awesome, was it safe* or *what the heck have I gotten myself into*—but there I was and not the youngest guest either. There were married couples, two with babies, as well as some older single travelers. The guests were not your typical college backpackers. These were all hardcore backpackers. In fact, I was not even sure if they were actually guests or people who checked-in many moons ago and just never left, but it was clear that I was the only guest without a tattoo and a body piercing.

The lodge was on the side of a hill and overlooked the ocean. The forest and the fine white sand on the secluded beaches were drop dead gorgeous. You could not see the lodge from the beach as it blended into the lush green forest. You could say the lodge had gone "green," but that would predispose it was something different at one time. At check-in, I noticed the lodge had a huge fire pit, a menu with food

which seemed appetizing, some local beer on tap and a sign next to the bar stating they had a poker game scheduled that night. Check-in also had a sign-up for the next day's "daily excursion" (more on this later).

The outdoor bar in Port St. Johns.

On my first night, I ordered the fresh fish of the day and a cold beer all for about $8 (US), and when you add in a fire pit and some very interesting people sitting at the community table, all was good. One couple had hooked up a few months ago in southern Africa. The guy had a Ph.D. from the University of Michigan, and the girl was an engineer from France. They planned on being on the road for a total of 18 months (or until their money ran out or they got tired of each other, whichever came first). They were all having a blast traveling. This group of wanderers had definitely put a hold on corporate life. The stories they told of places they had been and crazy people they had met, especially on the oversold buses they took between countries, kept me captivated all night. It made my Gap Period seem like a trip to Disneyland.

The smell of pot lingering in the air, the fun crowd, the innocent poker game and the fire pit aroma was not what I expected. A chill feeling ran through me like never before. However, youth and hardened backpackers definitely had an advantage over me when it came to staying up late and drinking. It was close to midnight and I knew I had to get some sleep. My room was cold and the cement floor had that wet, damp feel to it, and I could only imagine the types of bugs that roamed my room after dark. It was definitely not a five-star hotel, nor a three-star hotel. But I had an atmosphere that no fancy hotel could ever beat.

PLEASE DO NOT FLUSH THE FOLLOWING:

Tampons,	Maxi Pads,	Cigarette Butt
One Night Stands,	Cell Phones,	Condoms,
Love Letters,	Junk Mail,	Rabbits,
Sweaters,	Socks,	Hopes,
Goldfish,	Dreams,	Diapers,
Makeup,	Wallets,	Maps,
Gum,	Poetry,	Babies
Puppies,	Hair,	YOUR EX

The backpacker lodge restroom rules.

Canoe Trip with Backpackers

I signed up for the four-hour daily excursion of canoeing (lunch included). The excursion was to begin at 11 a.m., but since we were on "African time," we actually left at 12:30 p.m. and came back at 7:30 p.m. In between, we went to where the movie *Blood Diamond* was filmed and then to a lake where we went canoeing. The lake was high above the ocean and deep in the mountains. As we canoed, MC, the tour guide, started a fire and warmed our sandwiches. We gathered around the fire to warm up from a brisk cold day on the water. The sandwiches turned out to be absolutely delicious, probably the best I ever had.

Beer was included and the drinking started well before we even left the lodge. I can only drink so much until I can no longer get a buzz, but it seemed like everyone brought along their pot to help keep their beer buzz. Not that I pulled a Bill Clinton, but I did have a momentary thought that maybe the sandwich was totally awesome for other reasons.

In SA, when you don't know someone's name you refer to him as "uncle," and the guys on the tour referred to me as uncle. They also thought I was in my early 40s. I guess traveling makes one appear younger. MC was interesting to talk with. He was in his mid-thirties and was an investment banker from Joburg. He was also taking a time-out for a year or so from the corporate world. He told me he had become consumed and overwhelmed with the 24/7 of corporate life and needed a time-out. He loved his current gig of meeting travelers and exploring the Wild Coast. I could tell he enjoyed hanging with a bunch of lost souls who enjoyed sharing pot and getting stoned.

When I returned to the lodge, I received a call from a lawyer at my Firm. This particular lawyer and I always had good conversations—even if I did all the listening (I guess that sort of qualifies as a conversation). He learned of my Adventure and wanted to know how I planned it, but more importantly, pulled it off. He was interested in doing the same. Well, he was 67 years old at the time and one of the top paid partners and was asking *me* how to leave the Firm? This conversation confirmed how addicted people are to work in every age group, and it is difficult to leave no matter how much you make, save or receive from a monthly pension. After a day of hanging with a group of lost, pot-smoking souls and drinking beer on a lake on the Wild Coast, this conversation brought a smile to my face and validated what I was *experiencing:* living a life full of adventure and excitement.

Three days was the perfect amount of time to stay in Port St. Johns with terrific, and ever so interesting, backpackers. We had fun canoeing, playing pool, staying up late and drinking beer while staying warm by a fabulous fire pit. I came to love eating meals at the community table since they always produced interesting conversations. What I found most interesting was that many of the backpackers were also taking a break from very successful corporate careers. They were stepping out and exploring life. It was nice to hear their experiences of transitioning to a non-corporate lifestyle for a period of time.

I was very impressed by how the Port St. Johns backpackers traveled. They were "experiencing" and not just "doing" life. They didn't wake up saying we need to see, see, see. They woke up and let each day unfold naturally. They were relaxed travelers. They *saw* more than any tourist guide can ever show a person. It made me think that it would be fun to take a few people on an adventure like mine. Maybe I could create a business for lawyers who want to escape Big Law for a period of time and don't know how. I can sell them this book and then take them on the very same tour I created. *Are you game?*

I left Port St. Johns for Durban with a big smile and many great memories. But I was ready to revert to a hotel with my own shower and clean sheets. And my Durban hotel did not disappoint. At check-in I was greeted with champagne, smiles and an overall tremendous welcoming attitude. Most hotel check-ins are pleasant, but at the Oyster Box, the process was over the top fabulous and welcoming.

A REFLECTIVE MOMENT: Along with the local paper, a quote from Virgil was at my door upon arrival: "They succeed because they think they can." This reminded me of the saying, "thoughts held in mind produce after their kind." I succeeded in creating this Adventure because I knew I could. I have always succeeded in life, notwithstanding that it may have appeared I was just "lucky" or "caught the right break." I succeeded because I knew I would. This may have something to do with my competitiveness. I want to win. And I do win. I never wanted to just bumble along in life and have what happens, happen. I never wanted to settle for C's in school. I wanted an A. Becoming consciously proactive with living was now my foremost goal. No more waiting around until my pension start date to begin living my life.

On my first morning in Durban, I had a great run on the beach that included a run through a jungle. The trees, the foliage, the streams and a muddy trail made for a surreal run, and I felt this overall sense of happiness. I was thrilled to have connected with many people on this Adventure, particularly those who were truly interested in what I was doing and with certain partners back at my Firm who supported my Adventure without even realizing it. Emails and FaceTime from friends inquiring how I was doing and where I was in the world (similar to *Where's Waldo?*) really made me feel great. Somehow, I knew my Adventure was touching people in different ways. I realized I could impact the world simply by becoming the person I was meant to be.

My Last Day in South Africa

I was feeling very blessed in Durban (and clean—I finally got the grit from the backpacker lodge off me). I was becoming more comfortable with my personal thoughts and the course my life was taking. The move from unplugging to never returning to Big Law felt better each day. Thoughts of what life would be like away from the day-to-day drafting of pension plans were becoming more realistic.

A REFLECTIVE MOMENT: Big Law does not teach or mentor one on how to be a successful lawyer. Lawyers in Big Law are simply expected to keep quiet and crank out billable hours. That was considered being a model Firm citizen according to the unspoken code. But taking an adventure allows one to see so much more to life outside of a standard sized office with a mahogany desk and a mug of Starbucks coffee. Waiting until age 65 to experience life is a waste of precious time. And all of us, to different degrees, run out of time.

Time to Cowboy-Up

On the eve of traveling to Mozambique (MZ), I became anxious about this next phase of the Adventure. Having to start malaria pills must have spurred this anxiety. I was concerned with the main side effect—hallucinations. Being around pot and its side effects were one thing, but I had no interest in experimenting with hallucinations.

A REFLECTIVE MOMENT: With each passing day, I realized how trapped one can become in a world of bill, bill and bill that is unconsciously chosen by lawyers. The pressure of satisfying clients, bringing in business and billing is playing the legal game at an incredibly elevated level. Absent an adult pause in this way of being, a lawyer will be driven to the severities of a monastic life.

CHAPTER NINE

MOZAMBIQUE

I went to bed worrying about my travels—the airport, my luggage, particularly my trusted guitar. I kept thinking, *What the f*** am I doing?* Nonetheless, I woke feeling alive. I was ready for amazing things to happen. As I packed, my eyes were wide open to the world, to life and to living it to its fullest. I felt I had actually become a modern day adventurer (or maybe I was experiencing the side effects of the malaria pills).

A REFLECTIVE MOMENT: One should not care whether people like or even understand what you are doing. It does not define nor determine whether you are a success. It goes back to Step #1—it is none of your business what others think of you. Dr. Johnson's view is that unless one asks another his/her opinion, their unsolicited opinion does not matter and should be ignored. This was my new attitude. If I needed validation for my Gap Period, I would still be back on the 47th floor doing the ERISA thing.

I made it to the Durban airport, checked my bags, made it through customs and received my VAT refund (via a prepaid Visa card that

I ended up losing, as I'm sure Visa was expecting). I waited at the gate enjoying my existence without a care in the world. The local papers were filled with articles about Nelson Mandela and his health and the fighting between his kids and grandkids who were suing one another. A few articles were about Obama and his promise to have better relations with all of Africa (and him warning Africa not to trust China). This was all drama I was addicted to through Fox News and CNN. I believe drama is an adrenaline hit like no other. But taking a step back from my *high station in life* and not fully understanding the Mandela family issues nor the US-African-China fears made me realize that getting caught up in news drama of the moment was a colossal waste of quality time.

While at the gate, I noticed most passengers were of the suits and briefcase type. The overweight bellies with ties ending halfway down those bellies were all I needed to conclude it was the morning flight into Maputo for work. No backpackers on this flight (they were all on a bus with their pot). There is a certain look about a business traveler. They are seasoned and efficient in what they carry on and what is checked. Most had that look—that George Clooney look. I struck up a conversation with a couple of businessmen who were on their weekly trip into MZ and then off to other parts of Southern Africa. These conversations made me thankful I was not on my way to a work appointment. The thought of trying to sell my services or fix an ERISA mess was too much to handle at that moment. I was warned, however, about malaria and the importance of taking my pills.

As for my MZ travel plans, all I knew was that the guidebooks raved about the beaches, and I was determined to check out the rave. Winging it in an unknown country added some serious excitement to my Adventure.

Pillow Talk

On the eve of my Adventure, I did something unlike me. I began writing a blog and updated it enthusiastically each day. It was really nice to know that people, beyond my mom, were actually following my Adventure and sending me personal emails about my travels.

One friend in particular emailed me that she read my entries in bed with her husband right before they went to sleep. I thought this was hilarious. My blog had become pillow talk.

The Fish Market

I survived the landing into MZ, made it through customs and to the hotel with no issues. The hotel was completely different from The Oyster Box in Durban. For one, no one said, "with pleasure," and more importantly, I was not greeted with a glass of champagne (yes, I had become spoiled with SA hospitality). Excellent service does go a long way.

After I checked in, I attended an intense CrossFit spin class taught entirely in Portuguese by an instructor who was just incredible. After her class, we spoke of travel opportunities outside of the city, and she gave me a good overview of places to check out. It was nice to hang out with her, especially once we exchanged water bottles for a glass of wine (or two).

The next morning, I struck up a conversation with two young Americans—a pair of suits—who worked at an NYC private equity firm conducting business in town. It was nice to briefly check into the crazy world of US business. This conversation cemented my decision of being completely done with that world. Listening to conversations about exploiting others for the sake of profits that lead to large year-end bonus payments was too much. The best part of my conversation, however, was the tip for lunch the "PE Boys" gave me—the *fish market*. They raved of their excursion so much that I was hyped to check it out.

Looking forward to a really nice seafood meal, I hopped in a taxi and headed to the fish market. As I got out of the taxi, I couldn't believe what I saw. This fish market was no Pike Place Market. It was located on a dirty and dusty lot that sold different types of fish—calamari, red fish, prawns, crab and several other varieties as well. As far as I could tell, none of the fish had ever seen ice.

I was attacked by 20 or so "helpers" all converging to assist me with my fish market experience. They offered to help me pick the best fish of the day. I decided to go with the first person who approached me and received the royal tour of the market. After 15 minutes of looking over the goods, he hooked me up with a cold beer and eight surprisingly delicious tiger prawns. A couple from Joburg sat next to me, and I had a really nice chat with them. He was there on business, and she (not sure if she was the spouse—I hoped she was—not sure anyone

would bring a date to this market) was along for the ride. Conversations with married couples, unmarried couples and unfaithful couples became a constant at lunch and dinner. And they always produced enjoyable conversations.

My lunch at the fish market.

The market was very interesting. People tried to sell me everything and anything—from peanuts to drugs, and I found it very amusing. I didn't stick around long after eating.

While walking around the main park of Maputo, I met a lady from the US Embassy. She was having lunch at a café and I joined her. She was in her early 40s, single and loved working at the embassy. I wasn't exactly sure what she did (she was very vague and after a while, I stopped asking), but she did look very official, with her crisp white blouse, sharp looking skirt and a US official badge attached to her waist. She had a sexy don't-mess-with-me vibe about her. It was not apparent if she possessed a gun, but I thought it best not to ask.

After coffee, we walked around the park for a couple of hours. She had been doing the embassy thing for quite some time and told me of all the various places she worked. We decided to meet later that evening for dinner at a little café located off an alley that I'm sure only the locals knew about. The seafood was incredibly delicious, and I enjoyed hearing more about her career and travels. We went for a stroll after dinner near the water and walked over to her apartment.

I was expecting to see a "safe house" environment but security at her place consisted solely of a lock on her front door. She said I had seen too many spy movies. As the evening came to an end, she gave me her embassy card in case I ever needed help. I wasn't the Jason Bourne type, but I took her card and thanked her for a great night.

A REFLECTIVE MOMENT: As one ascends the ladder of Big Law, life generally becomes predictable and routine. One becomes focused on the billable time, collections and realization percentages and large paydays become less of an adrenaline rush. Lawyers lose sight of who they are. Some can characterize an adult time-out as a midlife crisis or the like, but that conclusion is way too cliché for what an adult time-out is all about. Big Law lawyers have attained a level of professional excellence, and an adult time-out is simply a step in moving a career into a zone of genius. Some people believed my Adventure pushed me over the edge, and there was a possibility it had. But I was no longer concerned with living a life based on what others thought of my choices (Step 1). For the first time, I felt I was moving my life into the zone of genius. Wanderers make one interesting to the world, and more importantly, interesting to one's inner self. The confinements of Big Law and stepping out from one's high station in life may actually push you to flee Big Law. It had for me.

Risk More Than You Think Is Safe

It was quite the eight-hour experience to make plane and hotel reservations several hundred miles north of Maputo only by looking at brochures of hotels and villages and speaking with a travel consultant who spoke no English. I had no idea where I was headed, but I prayed that all was properly booked as the consultant returned my credit card. Nine days and a beach with lots of time to stay put and relax were what I needed. I had not been in one place for that long since the container ship days. It would give me a chance for a proper wash of my laundry (my clothes were tired of being washed in a hotel sink).

My Soul Awakened

In my first few days in MZ, I was feeling very much alive. An unexplainable energy flowed deeply within my body, and I could feel my soul awaken. Meeting adventurous people gave me a sense I had lived a claustrophobic life back on the 47th floor. The embassy worker was exploring life and the world while collecting a paycheck. She really expanded my sense of income generating possibilities outside the confines of the 47th floor. I realized in MZ that fleeing the billable hour lifestyle was ultimately the right move for me.

A REFLECTIVE MOMENT: Lawyers in Big Law do not have to follow the pattern of work, work, work, collect a pension (and social security if that will be around) and then go ten toes up. A separation from work, a firm and clients will allow one to focus on where you are, what you are up to, where you are headed and what you are being. It will lead to a course correction in life.

As the plane landed in Inhambane, I realized I was in the middle of nowhere. There was no security at the airport, and the landing strip was mostly covered with grass. As we walked across the cracked-up grassy landing strip, a handful of taxis were waiting in the hopes of taking someone, like me, to a hotel. A South African approached me and said, "Welcome to paradise." He offered to drive me to my hotel, and so I hopped in the bed of his truck and off we went. As he pulled up to the hotel, I realized my travel consultant did me right in terms of a luxurious hotel. I was booked at The Flamingo Bay Lodge. Once I arrived at the lodge I found an article that described it as follows:

> **Flamingo Bay Water Lodge is situated in the pristine bay of Inhambane, Mozambique. Flamingo Bay Resort offers luxury but affordable accommodation and is perfect for a romantic honeymoon.**
>
> Set in one of the most picturesque areas in Mozambique with spectacular views of pristine beaches and the crystal

clear waters of the Indian Ocean, this is an ideal holiday vacation destination.

The lodge is situated on stilts on the crystal clear waters of the warm Indian Ocean. This eco-paradise is home to flocks of flamingos, tropical fish and incredible sunsets that may be savored as another day comes to an end. The warm Indian Ocean offers safe bathing all year round, and the endless wide open beaches offer hours of strolling pleasure.

Exclusivity

This lodge is unique and the only one of its kind in Africa. Flamingo Bay prides itself in having an undisturbed eco-setting that is peaceful and pristine, and the lodge endeavors to keep it that way. Because of the setting and exclusivity, they do not allow children less than 12 years of age, allowing guests to appreciate the peacefulness, elegance and romance of this tropical getaway.

Honeymoon Destination

Flamingo Bay Water Lodge is the ultimate honeymoon destination. The chalets are situated away from the main building, adding to the experience of tranquility and serenity.

Okay. This is what you need to focus on: *a destination for honeymooners* and *no kids allowed*. And this is exactly what I walked into—a single guy among several honeymooners.

My hut was a standalone structure, literally on top of clear blue water with furnishings that were all first-class (like Four Seasons first-class). Each hut had its own ladder leading into the water where you could jump in for a swim or paddle in a canoe and a deck where I relaxed every morning, sipping on a cup of hot coffee, watching the sunrise, and was a perfect place to watch the sunset over the ocean with a glass of wine in hand.

The Flamingo Bay Lodge.

The huts were about 50 yards from the main reception area, and you needed to walk on narrow wooden rickety paths to and from the eating area. It made me wonder how often guests fell on their way to their hut after a night of drinking.

I quickly became friends with the Director of Food and Beverage and the Hotel Manager. As they walked me to my hut, all I could think of was how did I fit in this environment? I'm sure they thought the same. On the walk to my hut, they invited me to a beach party at a club called The Neptune that night. They told me that the club was located right on the beach, known for their pizza, poker nights and vacationers who were *not* newlyweds. I thought, game on!

Knowing that a night of drinking was ahead of me, I needed to get some dinner. The dinner special at the hotel was a dish called The Prodigal Son. I really like the biblical story, and could even relate to it, but that is for another book. So I ordered it hoping it would be nutrition for my soul. The Prodigal Son turned out to be a local fish that resembled a shark. It was garnished with vegetables and was absolutely delicious. A nutritious and/or spiritual dinner notwithstanding, my first night was all about the beach party at The Neptune. The club didn't have that honeymoon vibe nor any of the honeymooners, just vacationers looking for some fun under the bright, big moon on a deserted beach. Most of the tourists were from SA, and fortunately, some were single, around my age and were more interested in dancing on the sand than having shots of tequila. It was a great first night!

A Windy Night

Before I climbed into my mosquito net protected bed, I cranked the A/C. If there were any friendly mosquitos, I either killed them with cold air, or I froze them to the point they couldn't fly anymore. Either way, my first night sleeping in the hut consisted more of listening to the fury of wind blowing around outside than me swatting at kissing mosquitos. Luckily, in spite of all the hollowing wind, the hut did not move much. As much of an adventurer as I am, I had no interest in finding myself in the middle of the ocean come morning. As the morning sun rose, I pulled the curtains and watched a gorgeous sunrise. I sat on the porch drinking a nice hot cup of coffee while watching the sailboats in the crispy clear ocean. There was such an unexplainable peace in the air. I even felt my heart smile.

Live the Dream

I took an amazing four-hour quad/ATV tour of the surrounding villages during which I felt as if I experienced the soul of Africa. Interacting with locals who were curious about me was a great way to spend an afternoon. Each person I met was truly genuine, authentic and so inquisitive. We talked about nothing in particular but we all had many laughs.

These conversations moved me. I felt as if I really *saw* their life. Horsing around with kids and kicking a ball around on an empty dirt lot created a feeling of bliss, of truly connecting with them, and I

sensed an overwhelming peace among them. It brought a deep sense
of happiness within me, even if only for an afternoon.

At one particular
village, a sign read *Live
The Dream* above the
main entrance. *Live
The Dream* should be
a motto written in
a place where every
individual sees it each
and every day and
learns to take it on. It
became my motto.

Locals.

The town of Inhambane consisted of a few paved roads, and the
rest were covered with red clay. It reminded me of the French Open
tennis tournament. The majority of people walked everywhere and
very few had shoes. The women carried goods on their heads and
kids on their backs. But each and every person I met was completely
genuine, a quality that is difficult to describe with words. One local I
met three different times was a teenager who referred to himself as

Johnny Cash.

Johnny Cash. He was a young kid trying very hard to make a buck off a Westerner. Each time I ran into him I bought a cloth bracelet from him. He had great BS, and I must have paid $50 for three cloth bracelets. I asked if he knew any Johnny Cash songs, and to my surprise, he belted out "Ring of Fire" without missing a beat.

Becoming a Fifth Wheel

On the third night, I introduced myself to two couples (on their honeymoons, of course) who had been at the lodge for several days. One set was from Joburg and the other from Cape Town. I invited them to The Neptune for another beach party that night that the food and beverage guy invited me to earlier. And they were up for it.

After dinner, we headed to The Neptune. Unfortunately, it was dead. The bartender told us the party had moved farther down the deserted beach. And it had. The music was loud, and the bar was filled with people dancing and drinking. Besides hanging with newlyweds and feeling old, the scene was actually pretty fun. The couples were awesome and were clearly over the initial "newlywed activities" since they were willing to party with the new single guest—me. Everyone danced under the stars. Around midnight, the newlyweds wanted to get back, and we walked for an hour on the deserted beach back to the lodge. It was pitch black except for the shining stars. We witnessed the most spectacular shooting star any of us had ever seen. It was an awe inspiring and tranquil moment. We arrived safely, but sandy, back at the lodge. It seemed, however, the party had just begun.

The younger of the two couples invited me back to their hut for a drink. We sat out on the porch, overlooking the star-reflecting water just talking. We laughed about the strangest things, like how Americans say "BBQ" (a briar), "honking horns" (tooting) and "stoplights" (robots). They were also curious about my travels and my writing. I explained the purpose of my book, my blog and generally why I am on this Adventure. The conversation went something to the effect of (a) young professionals have yet to attain a perspective of how work can suck the life out of a person and (b) people generally think what I am doing is good for me but not for them. It seemed to them (and many other people) there was never a good time to take a break.

My conversation with this couple reminded me of a saying about regrets: *a man knows he is old when his dreams become regrets.* I am convinced that most people, by the time their social security benefits kick in, regret not taking time off in their pre-retirement years. I plan on not having regrets.

One day, I took a sailboat tour with a group from the lodge. The destination was Pansy Island. It was a cold morning to be on a boat, but I was up for an outing. The only other single person on the boat was a law student I met from India. She was in her early 20s and was traveling with her parents. I first met her in the lobby area while we were both on our computers. We were laughing and generally having a good time when her father approached and asked her in a stern manner, "Where have you been?" Boy did I feel like a schmuck. It was all innocent, and once the dad realized I was not hitting on his daughter, he relaxed and joined in on our conversation. It turned out her dad was a client of my Firm, and the daughter was familiar with my Firm as well. What a small world!

Once we arrived at Pansy Island, we all jumped in the water in search of the Pansy Shell. Pansy Shells turned out simply to be sand dollars. A family from SA collected tons of them. I collected none. On the way back, they told me about the story of the Pansy Shell

Pansy Island.

and suggested I google it. I did, and the legend goes like this:

There is a pretty little legend
that I would like to tell
of the birth and death of Jesus
found in this lovely shell.

If you examine closely,
you'll see that you find here,
four nail holes and a fifth one
made by the Roman spear.

One on each side is the Easter lily,
its centre is the star,
that appeared unto the shepherds
and led them from afar.

The Christmas poinsettia
etched on the other side,
reminds us of His birthday,
our happy Christmastide.

Now break the center open
and here you will release
the five white doves awaiting
to spread goodwill and peace.

This simple little symbol
Christ has left for you and me
to help us spread His gospel
through all eternity.

So there you go. Something new I learned while off the coast of
MZ.

An Afternoon with Newlyweds

When we returned from Pansy Island,
I opened a running tab at the bar and
began ordering champagne in celebration of the newlyweds. Since joining
the running club back in Houston, I
have come to appreciate the taste of
champagne. The five of us spent the
afternoon hanging by the pool, drinking
champagne, without a care in the world.
It was so much fun.

The food and beverage director.

After dinner and a well-needed rest from champagne, we all met back at the bar. This time we had my buddy, the food and beverage director, act as bartender. The dad, mom and daughter from India joined us as well. Since the dad was a Firm client, my initial reaction was to pick up the tab and charge it to client development.

The post dinner party went on very late. We were having all sorts of drinks *and* shots. Even the food and beverage guy joined us after his staff left for the night. The daughter had connected her iPhone to the speaker system, and we were blasting some hip Indian music. It was a good thing the huts were 50 yards away. It was a night of pure fun.

A REFLECTIVE MOMENT: Recently, someone made an offhand sarcastic remark, "It is not always about you." I don't remember the context of why it was said, but I remember the words. Why not make it about me? Lawyers generally live to the expectations of client demands, and only client demands. Lawyers should learn to take a step aside and include themselves into their own lives. We should acknowledge that we will say and do stupid things, but we should correct all mistakes immediately and then move on. The risk of being stupid and foolish is a lot more fun than being reserved and sitting on the sidelines of life with the corporate suits. Real change will materialize as we become the person we are meant to be.

The Empty Meaninglessness of Life

While sitting with a cup of coffee watching the early morning sun (and nursing a hangover), I realized that I had created a life full of work and no room for anything else. There was no possibility for anything "different" to unfold in my life, particularly because of my blind commitment to billing hours. But now with a commitment to explore the world, my life was open to all possibilities. I was ready to answer the call of adventure.

A REFLECTIVE MOMENT: Consider that life is like a bowl of cherries, and until it is emptied, it will always be just that—a bowl of cherries. Embracing "emptiness" as a way to create expansive possibilities in one's life allows an exciting future to truly evolve without the clutter, stains and strings of the past. Most Big Law lawyers purchase "stuff" simply to fill closets and garages (and that is why the Container Store is so successful) and otherwise work just to pay property taxes. Unplugging from Big Law and leaving that "stuff" in the past will create excitement and adventure where before it could not exist. Although my Gap Period was certainly a tremendous adventure, it will not stymie my future. My future will be about living the life of the person behind my blue eyes. I was determined to live life so that when the time comes for me to face Jesus, he would not need to ask, "Why did you not live the life I created for you?" A stigma in Big Law is if you take a break, as I did, you're a quitter, and any prospective law firm will judge you as a flake or otherwise not dependable. How wrong is this thinking? It is the interesting people in life that succeed. Just like getting into good law schools. Everyone has the grades and test scores to be accepted, but it is the people with interesting experiences that get the offer. It is the same in the world of Big Law. I had no doubt I would always be able to get a job no matter how much time I took off to be in this world. My experiences in life will be more than enough in landing my next job. Big Law will always want to hire me!

The Wedding Party

On the way back from a terrific two-hour brisk morning walk on a deserted white sandy beach, I ran into a wedding party. The wedding was the social event of the season, the buzz among the entire hotel staff and was taking on a life of its own. It was taking place on my last night at the lodge, and the bride and groom had reserved every single hut (and I was determined to get an invite).

I stopped at a beach bar for a bottle of water. It was about 10:30 a.m. and a group of 15 guys were already drinking. I put two and two together and realized this was the groom's wedding party. I struck up a conversation and told them how the staff at the lodge were all excited, and nervous, calling the wedding, the "ceremony of the summer" but more importantly, I let them know the lodge had ordered lots of alcohol—just for them. That made everyone feel very relieved. The guys, all in their mid to late 30s, were from all over the world and converged onto the beaches of Inhambane to have a fun celebration.

They were very curious about what I was doing in MZ all by myself. All of these guys had professional careers. Some were accountants and others engineers. The groom was a KPMG tax auditor and had previously worked with my Firm (again, small world). I told them about my Adventure, and they all related to my "time-out." I truly enjoyed when people understood that a week of vacation is not unplugging from corporate America. After my water had turned into some beers, our conversation continued about how people often fail at balancing life with today's demands of a professional career. This was so apparent as we laughed at the irony of talking about taking a break while each of us was monitoring our BlackBerries sitting on a beach in paradise. Each guy appeared envious of the solitude of my container ship experiment, particularly when I told them about the peace one feels while sitting on the G deck sipping a beer with a guitar in hand.

Before leaving, the bride and her party showed up unexpectedly. The bride was not exactly happy with the state of soberness of the guys. However, no one can stay upset in paradise, including a bride. The ladies joined in for some lunchtime drinks, and before I knew it, I had an invite to that night's wedding party. I was pumped.

I returned from my wedding party beach beers and checked Outlook. I received the following email from one of the best marketing persons who told me she was leaving the Firm. She was always so very nice and helpful to me over the years.

> Hello! Hello! Well, taking a page from my friend Mark's playbook, I just realized I needed a break from Corporate America (and it will probably be permanent). The Firm has been wonderful to me, and if I had to work, I would stay here, but life is too short. I want to do so many other things: get healthy, spend time with my mom while she is still on this earth, finish the book for Book Club instead of just half, travel more, be present and

available to friends and family instead of distracted, be able to go to happy hour instead of working late, take some classes (maybe even some seminary classes), be a better helpmate to my husband and just float on my back in my pool. I have been so stressed out for two years, I don't even recognize who I am, ya know? That is probably TMI, but bottom line, I have been living according to the pressures in my world, not my priorities. And I decided to change that...

I have so enjoyed getting to know you, Mark. You are one of the most personable, authentic people at the firm. I love it that you aren't defined by your job and have sought adventure outside the tax code. I take your friendship with me as I leave the Firm—I'm not leaving the people behind. When you return, I'd really like to hear about your travels and see some of the pictures. Just don't make me run around Memorial Park before joining you for a beer. Please do let me know when you are back in town, and in the meantime, I will look forward to reading the blog!

Safe travels,
Nicole

It was nice to be acknowledged for the type of person I was and that I made an impact on at least one person by simply being me.

Be more like the man that you were made to be.
—Mumford & Sons, "Sigh No More"

A REFLECTIVE MOMENT: I have really enjoyed the music from Mumford & Sons. One of their songs, "Be More Like The Man That You Were Made To Be," hit a cord with me. For my entire career, I worked according to the Big Law code—keep your head down, do exceptional work, don't question Firm culture or its workings, and basically don't make waves. This was considered being a model Firm citizen. I grinned and bore it since that was the Firm way, and on one level, it was working. Grinning and bearing was less risky than creating change. But I was beginning to realize that in order to be the man I was made to be, I needed to up my game. We, lawyers in Big Law, are on autopilot to a certain degree in life—but no longer for me. Instead of blaming the Firm for the culture that was created a long time ago, I now get to decide how I want to be. It was my choice. I no longer needed to live as if I was trapped and confined to the walls of the 47th floor. I decided to wake up each morning determined to meet new and adventurous people. Convinced this would definitely happen had me pumped for the flight back to Maputo. I realized my historical way of planning, planning and more planning deprived me of all kinds of opportunities, especially of letting the unknown unfold before me. Allowing the unknown to reveal itself each day is a very exciting way to live.

The wedding event was more like a semi-mature bachelor/bachelorette party. They had the party on the beach with a blazing fire, a local guitarist playing music we could all sing to and alcohol that kept flowing throughout the night. Although the group was more mature than one would expect at a 25-year-old wedding party, maturity wore off, and craziness did take over as the night went on. Yes, people decided to swim. I warned them about *Jaws*, but they laughed as their clothes hit the sand and bodies hit the surf. I must admit swimming underneath the moon and stars was worth the risk of being eaten by a shark. We kept the fire going all night long and talked and laughed about nothing in particular. The hotel staff brought us coffee and muffins as the sun rose and our fire died. As we headed back to our huts, the sole single bridesmaid invited me to be her "plus one" for the wedding. I told her that I had some snappy Zegna clothes to wear and was more than happy to accompany her.

The wedding ceremony was a continuation of the fun we had the night before. The lodge was decorated with local furnishings—palm trees and other greenery. A bar made out of driftwood held the nev-er-ending supply of booze. The actual ceremony was very lovely, and tender vows were exchanged. I could feel their love, but as with all wedding ceremonies, the guests were ready for the reception to begin.

The reception was even more fun than the beach party. They had live music, limbo dancing and delicious food. As evening came and the music stopped, I was not shocked when we headed back to the beach with bottles of champagne in hand. We scrounged up some driftwood for another awesome beach fire, and not long thereafter, everyone hit the surf again. We did not make it to sunrise, but my first African wedding experience was super memorable.

Saying goodbye to the hotel staff at the Flamingo Bay was dif-ficult. The staff was not your typical Hyatt or Marriot staff. They were exceptional. They truly loved their jobs and the action of guests coming and going. They were fun to hang and party with, and they loved the beach. They were genuine people, demonstrating the fun part of work while treating guests with superb service, and then were off to a beach party. A perfect work/life balance.

As I waited for my plane back to Maputo, I emailed my US Embassy friend, Susan. I invited myself to hang with her that night. Well, to my surprise, she instantly responded and told me she was heading to a party with some friends and would pick me up at 7:30 p.m. sharp. I was psyched to have a plan for my last night in MZ. I gathered it would be a nice quiet get together, sitting around drinking red wine and chatting about US politics.

A Night with the Ambassador

Susan picked me up at exactly 7:30 and we headed out. The party was far from small talk, sipping on red wine. It was an incredibly wild night at an unofficial US Embassy party, celebrating an employee moving to Mumbai, thrown by the US Ambassador. Lots of food, drinking, dancing and loud music. I had never been to a going away party like this. There must have been over 100 people, and every one of them danced, sang and had a great time. The DJ played a mix of pop and local music that blared into every room in the house and the delicious food was prepared by the Embassy workers. I could tell that this office really enjoyed being with each other.

Hanging with this group of career federal workers made me wonder if I, a Type A person, could ever take up this type of assignment. One person I spoke with said he pretty much did nothing every day at work, and another said he met with local officials and sent reports to Washington. Sounded very productive! One woman who was there on a fellowship with an NGO dealing with HIV and related health issues enthusiastically explained the issues, problems and challenges facing MZ and its people. When I asked whether she and the NGO were making a difference, she said, "I doubt it, and that is why I am going to law school in the fall to become a Wall Street lawyer." This comment made me think that an embassy working environment may not be the right career choice for me. I'm not sure what time the party ended, but Susan and I left well after midnight and our government workers were still going strong.

CHAPTER TEN

A MONUMENTAL SHIFT: UGANDA

On the equator.

I never thought much of Uganda until I was looking at my bookshelf. I found an out-of-date travel book on Africa crammed among my other travel books, and when I opened the book, Uganda was the country that appeared. The Lonely Planet described Uganda as the *Pearl of Africa* and a top destination. I googled and googled and eventually found a tour for the last two weeks of July. I had no idea if I had just wasted $7,000 but a friend found the tour company on the Uganda BBB list, and this made me feel a little better about my choice. When booking the tour, they gave me the option of upgrading to luxury hotels for an extra $20 per night, and I splurged.

"What the F*** Am I Doing?" Revisited

I felt really good about my process of transitioning out of an intense career and in my decision to never return to Big Law. But as I sat crammed on a plane in my middle seat between two overweight and smelly people, completely exhausted on my way to the Pearl of Africa, I was having a *what the f*** am I doing* moment again. I had really hoped I was done with these types of conscious panic moments. But this time things were different. I felt as though a two-by-four hit me upside my forehead. I was emotionally overwhelmed with stark thoughts of *Am I crazy to give up a career I truly enjoyed? Should I abandon an ERISA practice I worked so hard to create? Why am I having these drastic reversals of thought? Am I missing work, my colleagues, my clients?*

I sat with a cold cup of coffee in my hand, snacking on stale peanuts, and I thought about how I really enjoyed the thrill of resolving complex ERISA issues for clients and working with brilliant minded colleagues. But more importantly, I thought about how I could create a work environment that would result in more attention to my current clients rather than concentrating on acquiring new ones. If I could focus my time, talent and specialized expertise on fewer clients and engage them in all the areas of law that my Firm has to offer, I would transform how I serve clients. This would be in my clients' best interest and at the same time would generate profitable revenue for my Firm. After all, 80 percent of my generated revenue already came from 20 percent of my clients.

I also knew I was no longer willing to be a part of the "work is hard, and the Firm is wrong" conversation. Big Law is challenging, intense and stressful but it can also be fulfilling and rewarding. Plain and simple. This new approach, a newfound wisdom (so to speak), would be the cornerstone of attaining a fulfilling and rewarding career.

Where did this new perspective come from? Did I need to unplug completely from the Firm machine, hit rock bottom with a commitment to never return to reach this point? Or maybe my experience of hanging with the workers in Inhambane, who truly loved their work and balanced it with fun and friends, was the catalyst for me to realize that a career could be more than a grind until 10 p.m. SportsCenter.

This new state of mind shocked my senses. I didn't know whether this was an internal panic, a fleeting moment of clarity or the path I was destined to walk. Someone once told me a miracle is defined as a simple change in perception—could this have been a miracle? As I sat shocked by my sudden desire to return to Big Law, I thought maybe, just maybe, a miracle had occurred. Without fighting this unexpected change, or even trying to understand it, I decided to go with what I was feeling and see where it took me as I headed into the unknown of Uganda.

As I shifted towards the possibility of returning, I became resolute that my work/life balance had to be different this time or it just wouldn't work. I no longer had an interest in drafting retirement plans for the next 13 years. I needed to reinvent myself and my ERISA practice. I began to think of the possibilities of how I wanted my work/life balance lifestyle to look like. I was convinced that my future in Big Law could not look like my past. As I journeyed into the depths of Uganda, techniques of how I could expand an already successful ERISA practice became a constant thought. I became jazzed about my career more than ever. I wondered, could Big Law indeed be a fun part of my life?

I was intent on taking my Adventure experiences and bringing them into my Big Law career. I would treat clients Inhambane style, just as the staff treated their guests—with superb service, and then come quitting time, rather than taking off for the beach, I would swim, bike and run. I would commit to approach each day expecting new and novel issues with clients. I would apply a sense of curiosity to my future within my Firm. A perfect work/life balance. It was clear I would, and must, bring this energy and service to myself, my Firm, but most importantly, to my clients.

I vowed to respond to each client's, "Thank you, Mark," with a, "With pleasure." I wanted to make each project more about resolving a client issue efficiently and cost-effectively rather than an exercise in billing hours. I intended to make each project a positive experience rather than a task that only generated cash.

I believe the key component to obtaining and retaining work is to continuously provide great service. Great service will generate more fees than any client entertainment trick. And it is just that simple.

Moving Into the Unknown

A REFLECTIVE MOMENT: I recently read a book titled *The Big Leap*. It's a great read about moving one's life from a "zone of excellence" to a "zone of genius." The author discusses how successful business people believe that attaining professional excellence is the ultimate goal in one's professional life, but actually, there is a higher calling—the zone of genius. He describes what blocks one from achieving this zone of genius and provides coaching tips to overcome these blockages. I want to reach this zone of genius. I was determined to transform my already established excellent game. I was committed to making my future not look like my past—I had already lived that. Few people would have taken an adventure in the middle of a productive and successful career, but this Adventure was the start of moving my life into the zone of genius. What this looked like or meant, I had no idea, but it was freeing to not walk into the past. Working for nearly 25-plus years at one job and attaining the highest accolades that an ERISA lawyer can attain (there are not many ERISA accolades so cut me some slack here) was achieving a level of excellence, and for most people, that is enough. However, I wanted a career in a higher zone—a zone of genius. This was my commitment.

Best Way to Predict Your Future Is to Create It

The tour I signed up for provided a brief summary of each day's activities that mostly matched my experiences. I have provided the "narrative," in their words, as an introduction to my daily Adventure.

Entebbe Airport Transfer to Kampala

Meet with a drive guide from Brovad at the Airport, and he will drive to Kampala, the capital city of Uganda, for dinner and overnight stay at Serena Hotel luxury/Cassia lodge for standard accommodation.

Expect the Unexpected—Uganda Tours

I arrived at the Uganda airport and made it through the customs and visa process with no issues. I landed around 7 p.m. and was completely exhausted but very excited and looking forward to a group tour. Solo traveling since May 6th was getting old, and group travel was sounding much more fun, especially if it meant meeting up with an adventurous woman. Joseph from the tour company, who was to be my driver for the next 16 days, picked me up at the airport on time. Someone once mentioned that tourists carry watches and locals keep time. Since Joseph and my watch were in sync, I took this as a good sign. He informed me that he refers to himself as the "father of Jesus" (because of his God-given name). As we waited for my backpack, he chuckled looking at my tired and smelly body (plus beat-up guitar case). We talked, and he mentioned how much he loved Fanta soda and drank it all the time. Going forward, I decided to refer to him as the Fantaman (he did not fit the "Joseph" type).

Traffic was miserable leaving the airport. The ride to the hotel was long, hot, dusty and at an extremely slow pace. Plenty of animals on the road, people everywhere, walking and/or biking. The sound of multiple car horns being pressed at the same time was maddening. It took close to two hours to travel 25 miles to a hotel that was not on my itinerary. It seemed I was traveling through the worst part of a third world capital.

On the way, Fantaman informed me that my Pearl of Africa Tour group consisted of only two people—him and me. I was extremely disappointed. I was really looking forward to exploring Uganda with a group rather than just a tour guide. But Fantaman assured me that once we left Kampala, we would meet lots of fun and interesting people at the lodges.

I was dropped off at the Serena Lake Victoria Hotel, located in the middle of nowhere on the shores of Lake Victoria. In addition to being the only person on the group tour, I was the *only* guest in this massive hotel. And I mean massive. I had never stayed at a hotel with three separate wings of rooms. Although the hotel was very impressive, I transferred to the city hotel where I was originally booked. I needed to increase my odds of meeting some adventurous souls.

Fantaman.

A REFLECTIVE MOMENT: An unexpected benefit on this Gap Period was that I was maintaining, and more importantly, growing a law practice from Africa. I demystified the commonly accepted belief that one needed to be in an office billing away to succeed at Big Law. I was a million miles away, and work was getting along just fine.

Breakfast at the city hotel was a spectacular feast. I invited myself to eat with a lady who was eating alone, and as we spoke, she told me she worked at the CDC. We had a great conversation about what the

CDC was doing in Uganda, diseases and how effective malaria pills really are. I can honestly say I have never had a conversation about sex and diseases in a detached and objective manner before. As she was leaving, I invited myself to dinner with her and two of her CDC colleagues for that evening.

The CDC employees were in their mid-thirties and loved the travel that came with their job. At dinner, I pulled out my malaria pills and asked whether they really helped in preventing the disease. The funny part of this conversation was they did not even take the drugs. However, they did inform me of all of the "problem" areas within Uganda and gave some sage advice to stay away from prostitutes. That advice was pretty funny and unexpected. They were dead serious, however, about this prostitute advice. They educated me on the strictly enforced policies hotels have—"no non-hotel guests allowed inside." They claimed that without these policies, the hotels would be flooded with prostitutes. That explained why there were only *suits* at the bar in the evenings.

On my first full day in Kampala, I had a guided walking tour of the city. I took in Mass at the main Catholic church, toured the local attractions and visited the main market for gifts and gadgets (aka junk).

My guide was a young lady about 30 years old, and I must admit, she loved hanging with a white guy from Texas. She had me by the arm the entire time. I didn't think much of it until she started getting teased by the locals. All in good fun.

My Kampala guide.

On my last night in Kampala before heading out on the tour, Fantaman arranged for us to go to a local jazz club. I was chilling in the lobby waiting to get picked up and watched guests come and go through the hotel's security gate. I noticed Fantaman, on the other side of the gate, with a woman dressed to the nines standing next to him. You could not help but notice her and her outfit. She had that short skirt and high heels thing going on as well as hot pink lipstick. I made my way past security, and he introduced me to Nina. Without pausing, he said Nina was going to accompany me to the jazz club. *Oh my God, what have I gotten myself into?* was my foremost thought. There was no mistaking who she was and what she was expecting to transact that night. I immediately thought about the CDC warnings.

We hopped in *her* Mercedes and went for a 30-minute drive through town. I was with a high-priced lady, and this was definitely not her first rodeo with a westerner. The drive to the outskirts of town was a little shady, but surprisingly, we went to a pretty nice jazz club. Overall, the music was good, and the Club allowed guests to get up and sing (some of whom were pretty good). We sat near the stage, ordered drinks and I tried to make small talk; however, she did not mince words. She was the real deal—my escort was there primarily for sex and did not care for small talk about my life or hers. This was completely crazy—*me* with a prostitute. I took a deep breath and committed to experience this night with a *prostitute* (without the sex part, of course).

In an attempt to get to know Nina, as the woman inside, I asked all sorts of questions outside of the scope of sex. I learned she worked at a local phone company during the day, but from time to time, Fantaman would ask her to go out at night with a client like me. She had a three-year-old daughter with a man from London, but they were not married. As the conversation continued, she always seemed to bring it back to some form of sex and what I wanted.

She was not interested in getting to know me—this was purely business, and trust me my feelings and self-esteem were not hurt. She asked if I preferred a woman who did not have kids and offered to call one of her friends who would be more than willing to meet me back at my hotel, or if I wanted more than one she would have her friends meet up with us. I could basically have had whatever I wanted.

I suddenly became self-conscious of what other people were thinking. Imagine this—a white 52-year-old Texan in the middle of Africa at a nice music venue with a woman 30 years younger, dressed the way she was, surrounded by other locals. Generally, I do not care what others think, but at that moment, I sort of did. She became more persistent with her desires, and I politely said no, no and no. Finally, I could no longer take the aggressiveness, and I told her I needed to get back to the hotel and get some work done. As I lay on my bed, alone, after my night with Nina, I was pretty amazed at how uninterested I was in sex. She completely exhausted me.

Leaving Kampala

Following breakfast, the guide will collect you from Serena or Cassia Lodge and then drive to the Murchison Falls National Park. The drive takes you past the Luwero Triangle, through the Budongo Forest in the western arm of the Rift Valley. You will be rewarded with splendid views of the countryside. Arrive in the afternoon and head to the summit of the falls to enjoy the breathtaking views of the falls and the surrounding terrain. You will marvel at the waters of the great Nile forcefully making their way through the small seven-meter gorge and drop below to more than 40 meters with a thunderous roar. It is such a marvelous sight! Dine and slumber at Paraa Safari Lodge for luxury or Pakuba Game Lodge for standard accommodation.

Fantaman arrived in a ten-year-old refurbished Nissan Quattro—that was my ride for the next 15 days. I was hoping it would hold up. I was sure wild thoughts ran through Fantaman's mind when he casually asked how my night was. I replied, "It was interesting, exhausting and not what I was expecting."

We were about 30 minutes outside Kampala when we suddenly pulled into a local car parts store to purchase some nuts and bolts for the unstable back left tire. The nuts and bolts were not organized in sealed bags like at an Auto Zone. Fantaman needed to dig through a miscellaneous box of leftovers to find the right size. As he was searching, I thought, *I am glad this happened now and not five days into the trip.* Next to the gas station was a butcher shop. Envision a hot, dusty, dirt-paved parking lot with meat hanging in a window of an eight by ten foot trailer (think of a rundown food truck without wheels) with no ice or any type of refrigeration in sight and a man with a machete chopping pieces of meat hanging from a hook for the waiting customers. Flies everywhere. That was the moment I decided to go strictly vegetarian for the remainder of my trip within Uganda.

A few hours later, a car pulled up beside us and mentioned that the rear right wheel was wobbling. We stopped on the side of the road, and Fantaman tightened the lug nuts on all four wheels. I guess no matter how often you tighten a broken wheel, a broken wheel is still a broken wheel.

As we searched for a gas station to get the wheel fixed, we drove through several small villages. In each village, the children at the local grade schools wore different brightly colored uniforms, and the children were everywhere. It was nice to see kids laughing, playing and bringing such joy to the world.

We finally found a gas station in a small village. I was having lunch and waiting for Fantaman to return, hoping the tires were fixed, and I had that *What the f*** am I doing?* thought again. I was four hours outside of Kampala and two hours from the hotel with a broken car. I was convinced I had totally messed up my career and for what? A trip to Africa? As I sat in a s***hole of a restaurant in central Uganda, I wanted nothing more than to be back on the 47th floor billing hours. This whole car business was turning into complete chaos. An Avis or Hertz right down the road was highly unlikely. I had no choice but to pray that things would get better.

The only way to get to my lodge was through the National Park. The entrance, however, was closed by the time we arrived. We paid the park rangers cash (and not under the table) and were able to get in, and more importantly, onto that last Nile ferry crossing for the day. Fantaman clearly knew how to maneuver within the bureaucracy of the Uganda Park Rangers. The ferry was not your modern day Staten Island type of ferry. The ferry was a wooden platform with a motor and a rope tied to the other side of a 100-yard river crossing. I was curious as to how they made this crossing work with the weight of four vans, several bicycles, some cows and a group of passengers. There was an upside to being on the last ferry for the day—I was able to witness a gorgeous sunset over the Nile. I felt like I was living back in the King Tut era for a moment.

Crossing the Nile.

Once off the ferry, it was a short ride to my first lodge. The lodge staff greeted me with a fresh glass of juice and a hot towel. It was truly awesome to be greeted like this. I was surprised at how nice my "deluxe" accommodation actually was—seriously! I walked around the grounds and took note of all of the "Beware of Wild Animals" signage and guards with AK-47s patrolling the grounds. I was told the guards were there to "scare" off raging elephants. Fear of raging elephants and AK-47s was enough to keep me on the grounds of the hotel at all times.

I had a glass of wine at the bar before dinner. As I sipped my wine, I noticed there were more guests here than in all of the hotels in SA combined. And they were all Americans (this was a bit of culture shock being with so many chatty and loud Americans). There were about 15 college kids sitting near the bar and some were pounding vodkas and the like. I struck up a conversation with them and learned that they were traveling with their parents on a mission trip. I chatted with some of the parents and got an invite to sit at the "adult" table for dinner.

I had never spoken with missionaries before, but our conversation was very interesting. The parents were very religious, taking their mission trip very seriously by preaching to the locals, especially the children, about the Kingdom of God. They spoke with passion for God and the projects they had worked on. They wondered why I was traveling by myself, and I told them my story about taking time off from work. In a New York minute they were discussing how I was doing God's work and how transformative my Adventure was from a religious standpoint.

It was a big leap to transform my time off into a religious pilgrimage. However, I became enthused with the conversation and considered the possibility they may be on to something. The discussion enrolled me at one level into the benefits and service this group provided. However, there was this nagging doubt in my mind as to whether they were *really* making a difference in the lives of the locals or were they here for a safari? As the evening came to an end, I was ultimately grateful to talk with some Americans and thanked them for the invite to eat at their table.

A Safari Day

Before sunrise, begin the day with an early game drive in the early morning to see the early risers plus the predators. Some of the animals you will see include jackals, giraffe, antelope, Uganda kob, hyenas, lion and elephants. Return to the lodge for a late breakfast plus lunch. Enjoy an afternoon launch cruise on spectacular Victoria Nile which will journey you to the spectacular bottom of the Murchison Falls seeing animals like buffaloes, hippos, crocodiles and elephants along the river banks and not to forget are the numerous aquatic birds like the uncommon shoebills plus the fish eagle. Dine and sleep at Paraa Safari Lodge for luxury or Pakuba Game Lodge for standard accommodation.

Following a stormy night with heavy rains, I went on my first African safari. It was awesome to see animals in the wild, and Fantaman was very good at locating them. Although I stayed in the truck at all times, Fantaman had a way, call it experience, of quietly driving up on animals without spooking them. It was quite amazing. We spotted lots of hippos, elephants, giraffes, lions, hyenas, warthogs, antelope and various types of birds. We even saw a kill by a lion which was very exciting. It was the whole circle of life right in front of my eyes.

At lunch, I sat with a couple from South Carolina. The wife was writing a book about their mission experience at an orphanage in Kampala. They were enamored with the pastor of the orphanage, which led to a conversation about life and work generally. I told them I was taking a break from Big Law, and she was all about the religious aspects of life. The husband was very cynical about my entire Gap Period and had mentioned, in no uncertain words, that the Firm was going to recoup from me "in one way or another" a price for allowing me to take my Gap Period. He was convinced that Big Law does not allow someone to take a break without a price being paid. He was clearly not the religious one in their marriage.

This couple, together with the mission people I met, had me wondering whether my Adventure may possibly be about God and serving his Kingdom. While riding a stationary bike in the hotel gym later that afternoon, I realized this was NOT what was going on. I was not in search of God, looking for meaning or the like. I was not quitting or retiring from corporate America. I was taking a break from what I had been doing for 25-plus years. Nothing more, nothing less. The more I thought (or dwelled) on these conversations, the more I realized it was simply another example of letting others dictate my thoughts and actions. At that moment, I wanted nothing more than to get away from close-minded people.

On the Move to the Primates

Enjoy breakfast and then cross with a ferry. Continue to Kibale National Park where you will arrive in the afternoon, have a delicious lunch and rest. Dine and slumber at Kyaninga Lodge for luxury or Primate Lodge for standard accommodation.

An Eight-Hour African Massage

We left the Safari Lodge at 7 a.m. sharp to drive to the location for tracking chimps. According to Fantaman, this ride was to be an

eight-hour African massage (aka driving over severe potholes and
terrible roads). My African massage in no way felt good, and in fact,
it was a miserable car ride.

As we were driving, we heard a loud bang. The right rear tire blew
out. It seemed a day in Uganda could not exist without a tire issue.
Thankfully, we had a working spare. As Fantaman was changing the tire,
the jack slipped, and the axle narrowly missed his head. Deep inside,

I knew the crush of
the wheel damaged
the brakes. I insisted
on helping him, and
with some finagling
of rocks, a log and a
rebuilt jack, we were
able to get the spare
tire on. We were both
hoping it would get us
to the next town where

Fixing a tire.

a proper mechanic
could fix it—again.

After a very long drive, we arrived at the Primate Lodge. The
accommodations were great. I was treated to sleeping in a huge tent
elevated ten feet off the ground. At check-in, they were adamant about
me zipping up my tent to keep the baboons out. Baboon warnings
notwithstanding, checking-in and getting a preview of chimp tracking
had me very excited. The chimps were definitely the star attraction
in this part of Uganda.

On the ride to the chimps, I casually mentioned to Fantaman that
I had met a group of missionaries that had just finished a mission
trip and were now on a short safari. He rolled his eyes and said,
"Mzungu, everyone has an agenda" (Mzungu is a local reference
to a white man). Fantaman said he sees all kinds of Americans
volunteering in orphanages and building schools, but they *all* have
ulterior motives. I did not want to get in a conversation about what
he actually meant, but I could see the disgust with these "volunteers"

on his face and heard it in his voice. Maybe they had stiffed him on a tip—who knows.

Tracking Chimps

After breakfast the next day, set out looking for chimps within the tropical wet forest of Kibale. As you look for this closely related species, you will come across other primates like the bush babies, mangabeys, the colobus monkeys and baboons. The guide will keep on educating you about the flora and fauna in this place and also brief you more about these chimps. This will be a full day in the forest to see how chimpanzees live in the forest. You will come back to the lodge at around 7 p.m. after the chimps go to bed.

I was in the jungle for eight hours with a guide who carried an AK-47 (in case we ran into raging elephants). Words cannot describe this experience. We tracked down a group of five males and followed them for at least four hours. As they slowly walked, we slowly walked. Not even my attempt to walk without making noise disturbed their peaceful afternoon. We even stopped and had lunch while they napped. They clearly knew I was there but were not bothered in the least. Being in a jungle with chimps ten feet away was an incredible way to spend an afternoon.

A chimp taking a break.   *On my walk with the chimps.*

A REFLECTIVE MOMENT: Unless you create a future of adventure, you will be collecting social security and wondering where life went. Accumulating stuff and achieving work-related goals is all about "doing." Be more than creating an impressive résumé full of Super Lawyer awards.

Preparing for a Climb

On the front end of booking the Uganda Tour, not knowing anything about the mountains in Uganda, I booked a weeklong trek in the Rwenzori Mountains. And the time had arrived for some altitude. So after hanging with chimps, I was off to climb.

Fantaman explained the climbing schedule a bit more, and I began to mentally prepare for the Rwenzori Mountain experience. He had cautioned me that these mountains would be more challenging than what I would experience on my Kilimanjaro (Kili) climb partly because of their steepness, icy trails and extreme cold. I had serious doubts about his assessment.

A REFLECTIVE MOMENT: The morning of the climb, I woke thinking about Big Law and how I would create a different experience. As I sat drinking coffee in the local village café waiting patiently for a 15,000-foot climb, the following came to mind:

1. During my 25-plus years as an ERISA lawyer, I had created a sophisticated and complex practice that generated serious revenue, but I was stuck in the middle ranks of the partnership. And by anyone's standards, I was not a middle rank partner. Successful lawyers who graduate at the top of their law school classes often resign themselves to simply becoming billing machines regardless of their talent to lead in the growth and prosperity of a law firm. I became determined (while staring at snow covered peaks) to up my game and lead my ERISA group to new heights.

2. In ascending to new ERISA heights, I pledged to transform how ERISA services are delivered. Focusing on fewer and more consequential clients, formulating alternative fee arrangements and taking on leadership as a way of "being" will be an example of how legal services will be delivered in the future.

3. Big Law must transition away from old school thoughts and

ideas created by lawyers of generations past and incorporate the new movements of the young. We must evolve as a business beyond the focus of accelerating collections of stale account receivables and instead create a new path to growth and revenue in a post-Great Recession era.

4. Big Law needs a "new thought alliance" among partners and the management team. Big Law leaders need to articulate a vision for partners that will attract, inspire and motivate all partners to take action towards becoming more than just billing machines. Creating new thoughts and concepts outside of traditional norms will drive business results, and revenue will flow into the partnership like never before. A new approach is needed—that is my bet.

So where do I fit into this vision for the future? I'm committed to my Firm, team and practice. I've decided to solely focus on my ERISA team and together with my associates, reach new heights in the ERISA world. We would expand our approach to bringing in work. I would bring in clients with issues that our ERISA group traditionally avoided, such as financial institutions and complex ERISA investors. My ERISA group would soar beyond all expectations and become noticed as a leading practice area. I was no longer willing to be pegged as a middle-of-the-road, service only partner.

Trekking the Mountains of the Moon

After breakfast head to the Rwenzori Mountains National Park Head Quarters at Nyakalengija (1,646 m.). You will receive the briefing from guides with the possibility of renting equipment. The hike starts through the plantations and homes of the Bakonjo, the people of the mountain, gradually reaching garden plots and elephant grass. You follow the Mobuku River, until crossing the Mahoma River. The trail passes through an open bracken fern slope and podocarpus forest up to Nyabitaba Hut (2,652 m.), which is the arrival point for the day. This will take from five to six hours. From the location, you are facing the north of the Portal Peaks (4,627 m.) in front of Mount Kyniangoma. During the day, you might see monkeys, the Rwenzori Turaco and hear the chimpanzees.

Because in the end, you won't remember the time you spent working in the office or mowing your lawn. Climb that goddamn mountain.
                                        —Jack Kerouac, *The Dharma Bums*

I was really excited about seeing mountain gorillas, but what I really wanted was to get in some climbing. Because I was committed to climb Kili and step on the Roof of Africa, I needed some altitude training. I was convinced this "training session" was nothing more or less than that—a warm up in some unheard of mountain range. The Rwenzoris, as described in the guidebooks, are "legendary," "Mountains of the Moon" and the "source of the Nile." They are the tallest mountain range in Africa, and Mount Stanley is the third tallest peak in all of Africa. The many peaks are permanently covered with snow and glaciers, which is why crampons, ice picks and ropes were required in addition to a warm sleeping bag.

Rwenzori Central Circuit Trek
Day 1: Nyabitaba Camp (2,650 m.)

From Nyakalengija the starting point, you will hike through a thick tropical forest and climb up a steep ridge with fields of ferns up to the camp. This takes you four to five hours to hike. The camp is located in a densely forested canopy mixed up with podocarpus trees. View a variety of bird species, black and white colobus monkeys, blue monkeys, butterflies and much more. Duikers and mountain elephants can be seen by chance.

Day one of the trek started off in an unnecessary hurry. I was dropped off at Rwenzori Mountaineering Services (RMS—my guide service) two hours after the guide service people were expecting me. In other words, I was very, very late. My guide, the cook and four porters did not like the fact that we were getting a late afternoon start. We barely made the entrance into the park before it closed for the day. We were delayed because Fantaman wanted to explore the many small villages along the way. Apparently, few of his clients request this trek, so he was exploring a part of Uganda for the first time.

On the drive, Fantaman assured me of a summit attempt, a warm sleeping bag, gloves, boots, crampons, a trekking pole and all other required gear, but what I was provided by RMS was a hike of the "Central Circuit" which consisted of six nights and seven days of hiking, rubber boots that were two sizes too small, a thin layered sleeping bag and *no* summit attempt, *no* gloves, *no* crampons and *no* trekking poles.

The guidebook provided by RMS described the camping as comfortable. However, the guidebook was crystal clear that a warm sleeping bag, warm clothes, climbing equipment and a first aid kit were necessary. Boy, was there ever a miscommunication/misunderstanding between Fantaman and RMS with what I needed versus what would be provided.

I was a bit miffed about not going to the summit, but when I saw a family returning from their summit *attempt* and how beat up they looked, not smiling and completely exhausted, I was discreetly happy to pass on it. Besides, how hard could a trek in the Rwenzoris be? Well, I hate to lead with the conclusion, but the trek was the most remarkably difficult climb I had ever undertaken.

Simon, my guide, was an exceptional climber and very religious. I have done several serious climbs around the world, and I have come to know a good guide when I meet one. I took the religious talk at face value since all Ugandans appeared religious. Philip was our cook (a pretty good one too). He was always smiling and talking Ugandan smack (that I mostly understood). I also had four teenage porters who carried the supplies.

I'm not sure how I would have made it up and down the mountain if it wasn't for Simon. Climbing was a serious challenge, not only mentally, but physically as well. My body was a complete wreck at the end of each day's climb. As for my sleeping bag, it was paper thin, and I froze every night. And I mean froze! I don't even think Walmart sells a sleeping bag similar to the one I had.

My feet were killing me throughout each day. My "gum boots" (rubber boots) were too small, and every time I hit a rock, pain shot straight up my leg. The makeshift trekking poles were of little use with the mud, rocks and boulders that I went over, around and through. I was basically very under prepared for this trek.

I used the phrase "Praise the Lord" when I would trip or twist an ankle on the trail. Being around religious people, I thought it was best not to say f***. To combat the cold each night, I prayed for everyone in my life as I fell asleep. I convinced myself that if I froze to death, I at least wanted positive thoughts in my transition to Heaven.

Simon and Philip (kneeling, left to right) along with our four porters.

Do Something Different

Some (profound) thoughts I had while trekking in the mud and the cold:

> 1. Going on this Gap Period was the first major proactive thing I have *ever* done in my adult life.

> 2. I will not get stuck in middle management at the Firm. I will lead my ERISA practice to a new level of excellence.

> 3. Creating a predictable future was not for me. I would not perpetuate my past.

4. Since Jesus did not preach in his village, I needed to consider a move to the Firm's New York office.

Day 2: John Matte Camp (3,380 m.)

From Nyabitaba to John Matte Camp is a six to seven-hour walk. The trail takes you through the Kurt Schafer Bridge at the Mubuku/ Bujuku rivers confluence, bamboo, heather with moss forest up to alpine zone of the giant lobelias and the groundsel to the camp surrounded by heather trees. The heather trees make its own zone; however, you will find other species of trees like the St. John's wort, rapanea, giant lobelia will be found in this zone. Animals like the rock hyrax can be spotted or heard at night.

Day 3: Bujuku Hut (3,962 m.)

From John Matte Hut you cross the Bujuku River and enter the lower Bigo Bog, a grassy bog where you experience how to jump from tussock to tussock. You reach Bigo Hut and enter the Upper Bigo Bog, proceeding to Lake Bujuku, where it is starting the alpine savannah zone of little vegetation. You finally arrive at Bujuku Hut (3,962 m.). This day hike can take up to five hours. There you have a view on the peaks of Mount Stanley, Mount Baker and Mount Speke. From Bujuku starts the diversion for whom intends to climb Mount Speke. For climbing Margherita and Alexandra peaks, it is advised to proceed to Elena Hut for overnight.

At the end of each day's trek, Philip would immediately go to work cooking over an open fire pit. His specialty was a house salad and hot dogs, and I devoured each meal in less than a New York minute. The meals, although minimal, accomplished my main goal of adding as many calories into my system as I could. And at the end of each day, I needed the calories. As for the trekking, each day was between four and six hours long and presented more challenges than the prior day. I kept wondering when things would get easy and when the cold would subside (which it never did).

Cooking dinner in the Rwenzoris.

Day 4: From Bujuku Hut to Kitandara Hut (4,023 m.)

From Bujuku Hut you climb through moss-draped groundsel vegetation to Scott Elliot Pass (4,372 m.) the highest point of the loop trail. The path is very rocky and steep at the foothills of Mount Baker. Enjoy a spectacular view of Margherita Peak, Elena and Savoia glaciers and Mount Baker. You reach Upper Kitandara Lake through thick mud to Lower Kitandara Lake where is located Kitandara Hut (4,023 m.), Kitandara in the local language means "fresh field," as a cold wind is blowing into the valley. Time to complete the hike is about five hours. During this tract, it is recommended to check any sign of altitude sickness or hypothermia. From Kitandara Hut you can proceed for climbing the peaks—Mount Baker or Mount Luigi di Savoia and the peak Vittorio Sella.

You Need My Support?
Yes.

Day four's ascent was a nearly impossible feat. I have climbed quite a few difficult ascents, but this was by far the most ridiculously challenging section of mountain climbing in my life. It began with a straight up climb of nearly 600 feet. We should have used ropes and ice picks, but just like a warm sleeping bag, they were nowhere to be found.

We climbed over and around rocks, boulders and loose gravel. At one point, we climbed straight up a 50-foot wooden ladder that I prayed would not break (the ladder was made from broken tree limbs and old rope—no nails—we could

A ladder used on the climb.

have easily fallen to our graves). Simon was an invaluable guide. At times, he pulled me up. It was one step forward and two steps back while we walked on the loose rock, and to top it off—it was freezing cold (as the Day 4 note indicates, hypothermia was a possibility at this point in the trek. Fortunately, I did not experience this). I made the 600-foot climb in about two hours and was completely exhausted. My clothes were entirely soaked with sweat. The altitude at this point was close to 14,000 feet, and we would stay at this altitude for several days. After a short break (for some bread and water—no power bars in Uganda), and a quick change into some dry clothes, we were off for a three-hour gentle climb/trek to camp for the night.

At camp that night, after I put on more dry clothes, I hung with the porters around the campfire. It was by far the most communication we had during the trek. We somehow got on the topic of music and Michael Jackson. I don't know exactly what they were talking about, but I did understand they thought he had become a mzungu. It was a great laugh had by all.

Taking a break from the climb.

Warming up in the Rwenzoris.

Kitandara Hut to Guy Yeoman Hut (3,261 m.)

From Lake Kitandara you climb to Fresh Field Pass (4,282 m.), a long flat of high alpine mossy glades, before descending the circuit among rocky and boggy areas. The panorama is dominated by the glaciers of Mounts Stanley and Baker. A muddy trail leads to Akendahi, Bujongolo and Kabamba rock shelters, where starts the Kabamba Valley down to Guy Yeoman Hut (3,261 m.). This can take up to six hours. The hut is surrounded by a beautiful landscape of mountains, vegetation and rivers.

We arrived at a hut on a lake at the end of this day's trek. Tall trees reflected on the still water, and it reminded me of the lake in the movie *On Golden Pond.* It was an incredibly scenic and relaxing view. But for it being freezing cold, I would have gone for a swim.

I hung with Philip as he cooked dinner and our daily appetizer. He told me that he was getting married in the fall and had to gift many goats to his father-in-law. We both had some good laughs over this Ugandan custom.

Before falling asleep, I reminded myself of a conversation I had with Lou Whitaker, a famous US mountaineer. He theorized that the climbing you did as a young person were banked hours; hours that you can use later in life to extend an active lifestyle. I bought into his theory and began to consider the next several days of trekking as merely banking hours for my later years. With this in mind, the remaining days were not only put into perspective, but I looked forward to the difficulty of each day's climb, both mentally and physically.

Camp beside a beautiful lake.

Now a little bit about my gum boots. These were basically old-fashioned black rubber boots I wore when I was a little kid playing in the rain. The problem with my gum boots was that they were two sizes too small, but I needed them since we would trek through ankle high mud for hours at a time (this was one of the reasons they refer to this trek as the "Mountains of the Moon"). My toes were killing me. With two days left on the trek, I had enough. My toes could no longer take the pounding. Every time I would hit a rock, not even my "Praise the Lord" prayer relieved the shooting pain up my leg, and with each descent, my toes would jam into the front of the boot. It became way too much to bear. So I reverted to my trekking boots and I dealt with the mud as we trekked along. By the time I was done with the Circuit, I had ten completely black toenails.

When we first began the trek, a porter mentioned the possibility of finishing a day early, but I didn't understand what he meant. Now, I clearly understood what getting off the mountain ASAP meant. Before falling asleep in complete exhaustion, extreme hunger and of course, freezing cold, I began to consider getting off the mountain one day early. In order to do so, it would make the last day of trekking a ten-plus-hour day. Now I am the type of person who wants to get his money's worth, and the thought of cheating myself out of a day on the mountain a week earlier was out of the question. But in that moment of complete exhaustion, hunger and cold, finishing a day early was the right decision.

Day 5: Kitandara Lakes Camp (4,027 m.)

From Elena Camp to Kitandara Lakes Camp will take you three to four hours to hike. The camp is surrounded by senecio/groundsel trees, lobelias and St. John's wort. While at the camp you will be able to see two beautiful upper and lower Kitandara Lakes. And you will have a nice view of the Elena Glaciers from this camp.

The day began with a trek directly up the side of a three-foot wide ridge at 12,000 feet of elevation. I was climbing on all fours, and I never declined an offering hand from Simon to help keep my balance (and of course from falling to my death). We then trekked straight down a valley. Again, an incredible challenge for six straight hours. Mountain guides have attained a level of fitness I can only dream of. At this point, I was hoping their assessment of these mountains being more difficult than a Kili climb was correct because if they were wrong, I would not see the Roof of Africa.

Simon and Philip made a visit to my hut just before my head crawled into my thin sleeping bag for another long, cold and miserable night, and I told them I was willing to forgo a night in a hut for a ten-hour descent, plus a hot shower. I was done with this type of fun.

Guy Yeoman Camp (3,450 m.)

From Kitandara to Guy Yeoman is five to seven hours. Descend after an early morning thigh bursting climb leads you to the Fresh Field Pass

(4,280 m.) to have a view of the Edward Glaciers on Mount Baker, Luigi du Savoia, Lakes of Kitandara and the eastern part of the Democratic Republic of Congo. Guy Yeoman is located within a scenic valley of River Mubuku, Bujongolo, Kendahi rock shelters of the Duke of Abruzzi and Kabamba waterfalls are part of the amazing attractions you will enjoy as you descend to this camp.

Guy Yeoman Hut Back to Nyabitaba Hut (2,652 m.)

In this day, you complete the central circuit by going back to Nyabitaba Hut. The trail is attractive along the valley of the Mobuku and Kichuchu rivers, rich in plants and flowers of the heather zone, before reaching the bamboo forest. See Kabamba Falls on the way. Time to reach Nyabitaba is about six hours. Eventually, you decide to terminate the trail by descending directly to Nyakalengija, adding two to three more hours.

The first two hours of the last day were totally taxing. It was the hardest part of the climb for sure. Thank goodness for Simon's help. He mentioned this part of the Circuit was the *"You are welcome from the Rwenzoris"* to every climber. He mentioned that men have offered their firstborn to be carried down this section, and now I knew why. It ended up being a 12-hour day. The first two hours of the descent involved scrambling straight down (and I mean straight down) over huge boulders and down wooden ladders, again made from branches. Ropes should have been used in certain sections. Then it was walking through freezing streams with lots of thick mud. The steepness of the descent was the most challenging *and* dangerous part, but I constantly reminded myself this was good practice for Kili.

After eight hours of descent, we ate lunch at what was previously a planned stop for the night. I wanted off so bad that adding four hours to the climb was well worth it, regardless of the exhaustion I felt from trekking these last eight hours. I was mentally and physically exhausted and ready to be off the mountain.

Following a brief late afternoon lunch consisting of water, fruit and bread, I gave the porters a tip for their incredible help and great attitude on the journey. They were the happiest four Ugandans. It was a delight to see their faces light up. I was curious where four teenagers spend money in a village with no apparent place for teenagers to hang out. But Simon informed me that they had plenty of places to spend cash and that it was a huge windfall for each of them.

Getting off the mountain a day early meant I needed a place to stay. When I arrived in the village a week earlier, there were no signs of a motel, hotel or even a hostel. In fact, there were no tourists. But Philip assured me that he had a place for me to spend the night. My imagination went wild. A place with no doors or windows were my initial thoughts. At least I would be off the mountain and not in a thin sleeping bag.

Philip was true to his word. I stayed in a lodge he operated and owned in some respect. My first order of business was a hot shower. The shower was disgusting. It was located in a partially enclosed open-air bathroom with huge mosquitos everywhere. I seriously prayed the malaria pill residue remaining in my body would prevent me from contracting this disease. I actually clasped my hands and prayed for it. The hot water was also lacking, but I did the best I could to get a week of grit off my body.

My walk up a 50-foot hill for dinner was extremely painful. My legs were killing me. However, my need for food outweighed the pain I was enduring. The Rwenzoris had completely wrecked my body. It was even more painful to stand up while getting out of a chair. I had to embrace the "slow is smooth and smooth is fast" approach to getting to dinner.

The cook was a cute and extremely bubbly 25-year-old local lady who also joined me for dinner. It was just the two of us in the restaurant, and we had a good chat about life in Uganda. She was not married but was in the market for a husband. *And she was not a prostitute. And I was not a husband candidate.* Dinner was great (as well as the white wine), but my entire body hurt too much, and after a glass of wine, I was ready for bed. As I drifted off to sleep, I reminded myself this was indeed an adventure, and I would not change anything notwithstanding the pain I was experiencing. I prayed that night: *Dear Lord, please do not let me contract malaria from any of these bugs that are renting* *the room with me. Please give my legs the strength to stand in the morning...*I don't even remember falling asleep during my prayer session. I was downright exhausted.

Nyabitaba to Queen Elizabeth National Park

Picked up by your driver and taken to Queen Elizabeth National Park situated in the shadows of Mount Rwenzori. The voyage will present exciting game drives along the way. Some of the animals to watch out for include: leopard, elephant, lions, buffalo and water birds. Arrive in the afternoon at the park to have lunch, and then continue for a thrilling launch trip along the Kazinga Channel. You will see thousands of hippos, aquatic birds plus buffaloes on the shores. Dine and sleep at Jacana Lodge or Mweya Safari Lodge or Ihamba Safari Lodge.

On the morning after my climb, I hopped on Philip's motorcycle and went to the local Catholic church for Sunday Mass where every seat was taken (I think the entire village was in attendance). The parishioners seemed mostly under the age of 45. The women were dressed up in bright dresses and looked amazing. I received lots of stares from people, especially the kids, probably because I was tall and the only mzungu at Mass. It felt great to be there. It was uplifting, and I was inspired. There was a lot of singing and clapping during the two-hour Mass that concluded with a 30-minute town hall meeting. At the end of Mass, the priest asked me to stand and be acknowledged. Life felt great. Afterward, I hung around outside and spoke with the locals and played with the kids. It was a great post-Mass environment, not like a typical US Mass when everyone, me included, walked to our cars and headed off to the business of the day. It would be nice to recreate this post-Mass atmosphere back in Houston. After 45 minutes or so, I hopped on Philip's motorcycle for the 30-minute ride back to my lodge where I was hoping Fantaman was ready for the drive to the next lodge.

To my surprise, Fantaman was at the lodge and ready to go, and to further my surprise, he had his oldest daughter with him. She was 18 years old and was going to spend a few days with us. I thought having a third person would be fun.

Wildlife Tour of Queen Elizabeth National Park

Begin the day with a game drive in the early morning to see the early risers plus the predators. The drive is so interesting with sights of bushbucks, hyenas, elephants, bush pigs, lions, buffaloes and jackals. Following the drive, return to the lodge for lunch. Afterward, proceed to the Kyambura Gorge to trek chimpanzees. This walk will present sights of baboons, black and white colobus monkeys and red colobus monkeys. Dine and slumber at Jacana Lodge or Mweya Safari Lodge or Ihamba Safari Lodge.

Elephants blocking the road.

We left the Rwenzoris and headed to Queen Elizabeth National Park. The park was nice and the wildlife good. That night, the three of us had a nice dinner. The only other guests at the lodge were a group of birdwatchers, consisting of 20 or so people, mainly from CA it seemed. The head birdwatcher and I struck up a conversation about our travels while waiting for dinner. He was quick to tell me that (a) he was from California and (b) he detested the Texas governor (Rick Perry). *Wow*, I thought. What a way to start a conversation. Without hesitation, I sarcastically shot back that I did not care for his governor (Jerry Brown). After I said this, his neck stiffened as he turned in a huff to rejoin his birding friends. Now I don't particularly care for politics but for some reason, being in Africa, I had that "Don't Mess with Texas" attitude going.

The Impenetrable National Park: Gorilla Trekking

Following breakfast, have a game drive on your way to Bwindi Impenetrable National Park. You will drive through the impressive Ishasha region prominent for its resident tree climbing lions. Check in at Bwindi, rest and later enjoy a community walk within the surrounding communities. Dine and sleep at Gorilla Forest Camp luxury or Silver Lodge for mid-range accommodation.

As we headed to the Impenetrable National Park, I was very excited for the highlight of the Uganda Adventure: trekking mountain gorillas. I couldn't wait to see a big silverback. First, we had to travel to a small village to drop Fantaman's daughter off at a bus station for her ten-hour trip back to Kampala. We arrived at the "bus stop" 30 minutes ahead of schedule. This bus stop was only known to the locals because there was no sign whatsoever indicating a bus was to stop. As we waited, a 20 something-year-old kid drove up and parked his car near ours, blasting music. The song "Call Me Maybe" came on, and I laughed knowing that he probably had no idea what the song was about (nor how the music video ends), but I started to dance with a few nearby kids on the dirt road in the middle of nowhere. I was sure I annoyed the super cool kid, but the kids had fun (and so did I).

We waited along a dusty road for about an hour before Fantaman decided that we should drive down the road to the next scheduled stop. After two hours of more waiting, an oversold 1970 Greyhound-looking bus finally arrived. That bus would have violated every transportation law in the USA; nonetheless, everyone somehow boarded. Fantaman apologized for the wait, but I was just glad to be back on the road and on my way to the gorillas. Fantaman, as a token of appreciation for my patience with his daughter's bus delay, allowed me to drive for a few hours—now that was fun! Trying to avoid huge potholes and various animals, including a herd of elephants, made the drive exciting. We also spotted some tree climbing lions. We were able to get directly under a huge tree with seven lions looking down on us through the sunroof. It was, personally, a little too close for my taste.

After a couple of more hours of an African massage, we made it to the lodge for the next day's gorilla trek. The driveway was incredibly steep and went through a thick deep green forest on the side of a rugged mountain. We had discussed meeting in the village that night for dinner, but after driving the meandering curves up the dirt road to the lodge, I had no interest in walking back down in the cold and damp darkness of the night. A glass of wine and a nice dinner at the lodge was perfect for me.

I spent the better part of the afternoon sipping tea and writing in the outdoor lounge area while occasionally staring out at the majestic mountains. These mountains were mesmerizing. Thirty minutes would go by without my eyes leaving them. Watching the mist rise from these purely green covered mountains was spectacular, and I couldn't believe I was surrounded by this natural beauty.

Is Your Dream Next?

While sipping tea, a mother and daughter from the UK sat down, and we struck up a conversation. They had returned that afternoon from trekking the gorillas and had nothing but great things to say about their experience. We conversed for hours. They were genuinely curious and impressed about my Adventure and asked many questions. However, they were all too quick to interject "I could never do this" or "Can you imagine Dad doing that?" It was strange to hear such statements because I had become convinced that everyone has the ability to take an adult time-out.

A REFLECTIVE MOMENT: I strongly believe everyone should take an adult time-out at some point during their career. Plain and simple. All I was doing was taking a pause in life. My adult time-out gave me time to step outside my legal career, rest from its intensity, reflect on what I created and become determined to move an excellent ERISA practice into the zone of genius. An adult time-out will result in a transformative career.

Mountain Gorilla Tracking—Lake Bunyonyi and the Switzerland of Africa

Wake up to an early breakfast then proceed to the park head offices for a briefing prior to entering the forest in search of mountain gorillas. By 9 a.m. you will start out in the forest. The activity is quite unpredictable but lasts from two to six hours based on the gorillas' movements. Gorilla tracking involves trekking steep rocks and moving across the undulating terrain. Nevertheless, the excitement of coming face to face with the gorillas will rob you off all the tiredness and reward you with wonderful memories. After gorilla tracking, you will head to Lake Bunyonyi. This is a very spectacular destination with beautiful small islands and enclosed by steep terraced slopes. It is renowned as a birding paradise with several aquatic birds. The lake was named Bunyonyi to mean the small birds. Dine and sleep at Birds Nest Lodge or Arcadia Cottages.

The day for my gorilla trek had arrived. I was extremely excited. I woke early and got some coffee in my system. I had my rain gear and a sack lunch ready and waiting for Fantaman who arrived in a very foul mood.

I was placed into a group of ten trekkers at the gorilla base camp. After hearing the rules of trekking (how to take photographs, don't try to feed or touch the gorillas and other common sense rules), we were off. On our way, the group stopped by the mandatory trinket store to purchase souvenirs (yes, the Ugandans knew how to generate income from tourists). I purchased a gorilla trekking pole (which stayed with me throughout the remainder of my Adventure) and attempted to purchase an "I've Penetrated the Impenetrable Forest" T-shirt but could not find my size. On the way to the entrance to the trek, I began to have an *it is time for this part of the Adventure with Fantaman to end* moment. I wanted no part of his foul mood, especially that day.

My fellow trekkers were all Americans. Penetrating the "Impenetrable Forest" was no walk in the park, especially for this group. It was a difficult trek up and down some serious terrain. One of the trekkers, a woman from New York City, barely made it. There was also a dentist from CA who had a camera that seemed to be five feet long, and he, and the camera, each weighed in at about 300 lbs. He struggled with the trekking (and with the camera as well). He purchased it solely for this trip, and I was not sure he really knew how to use it—but the flashy white and chrome camera did look impressive.

The guides would cut a path through the unforgiving and thick jungle with a machete, and we followed. It was surreal walking through the smell of newly cut jungle in search of gorillas. We trekked for three hours before all hardship was instantly forgotten when we encountered a gorilla family. There were about 20 gorillas with one very large, stern and scary looking silverback. It was like watching an extended family on vacation. The silverback hung out by himself and ignored the rest of the clan. The mothers took care of the babies, and the kids played and roughhoused with each other. Every once and awhile the kids would take one of the babies and gently toss him/her around. We were

allowed to get within ten feet of them, and they seemed not to care that we were looking in on their fun. After an hour (and a thousand pictures), the big silverback made a sudden charging motion toward us, which was frightening, and that immediately ended our visit. The gorilla family quickly followed the silverback as he made his way down the side of the mountain and into the mist. It was an awesome experience!

A silverback.

I was so stoked afterward. I witnessed something most people will never see. The trek in the misty mountains was like no other. Up and down and all around and then 60 minutes with some incredible creatures. Even Fantaman's ever increasing moodiness couldn't dampen my excitement.

My next lodge was located in the most southwestern part of Uganda where the weather was very damp and cold. As Fantaman ordered a Fanta and joined me and Patricia, the cook, to go over my dinner order, it became quite clear why Fantaman selected this lodge. Patricia had my dinner out in 30 minutes and then was off to meet up with Fantaman. As it turned out, Fantaman was not as religious as he led on; the daughter who traveled with us for a few days was from a woman other than his wife. Oh well.

Family fun.   More family fun

My lodge was located on Lake Bunyonyi (known as the "place of many little birds"), an incredibly beautiful lake with 29 small islands throughout. It is the third deepest lake in the world and on the list of the top seven Uganda highlights. The lake is surrounded by steep hillsides that were intensely terraced. It made me think of the terraced landscapes of Machu Pichu, the Cinque Terra and Nepal. It was a totally chill place to visit.

Lake Bunyonyi and Its Islands Tour—Lake Mburo National Park

Enjoy canoeing in the morning on this stunning lake to see the various bird species, and then set off to Lake Mburo National Park. This park is famous for its numerous antelopes among which are impalas after which Uganda's capital city was named—Kampala. Drive past breathtaking sceneries of the countryside to arrive in the afternoon at Lake Mburo National Park. You will break for lunch before going for a canoe ride on the Lake to look for the various animals on the lake shore. Dine and sleep at Mihingo Lodge luxury or Mburo Safari Lodge for mid-range.

After a restful and peaceful night and while sipping on coffee overlooking the calm lake, a sinking feeling came over me as I heard Fantaman's car come slowly up the driveway. He had become too much emotional work to be around.

Before leaving for my final lodge, we took a motored canoe ride for two hours on the lake. There was one island called Banishment Island where legend has it that unwed mothers-to-be were sent to give birth and die. The island was no larger than a small kitchen. We also stopped by a children's hospital located on another small island. The canoe

operator and I walked up and toured the hospital while Fantaman sulked in the hull of the canoe—he resented this stop (maybe his night with Patricia was not that enjoyable). This island reflected pure poverty. Plain and simple. Seeing sick kids, most without a parent, was very disturbing.

Fantaman.

On My Way to Kampala

Following breakfast head back to Kampala. Make a break at the equator to take some photos and visit the craft shop, and then arrive in Kampala in the later afternoon and drop off to Entebbe airport for the outbound flight to Kilimanjaro.

Before returning to Kampala I stayed at a remarkable lodge that in itself felt as if I was on an island. Each guest slept in a tent that was atop a wooden platform surrounded by zebras and antelope located in the savanna. The platform also had an amazing porch with a nice rocking chair where coffee was sipped while watching the grazing animals. There was an infinity pool at the main lodge as well. The pool, combined with a glass of wine in hand looking at grazing zebras was a beyond spectacular experience.

I spoke with one of the co-managers of the lodge before dinner and learned that she and her husband had a three-year contract to manage the lodge. I asked how they got the gig, and without hesitation, she told me to check out www.escapethecity.org. The couple was out to explore and experience the world before settling back in London to start a family. That part of the conversation was depressing considering the adventurous life they were living. I reflected, however, that returning to the 47th floor following my Adventure was really no different.

As dinner was being prepared, a group of eight of us from all over the world built a campfire. We had some good conversations about travel and how we all ended up in the middle of Uganda. It seemed like a combination of Google and guidebooks led us all to that fire pit. Two women from the UK invited me to join them for dinner, and that was super fun. We conversed about my Adventure, and the younger of the two (around 25) became so excited and enrolled in the "taking a time-out conversation," she began to plan her own journey. We also spoke on a wide range of random topics including the differences of being in this world versus getting things done. The older of the two was my age and ran a successful business in Kampala. She understood how corporate life, even in Uganda, can suck the life out of a person. I never tired of listening to people who understood what I was doing on this Adventure.

I made it to Kampala by early afternoon, and Fantaman dropped me off at my hotel. I gave him a generous tip, a high five and bid him farewell. The general manager of the tour operator, Fabby, who met us at the hotel, asked if he could drop by around 5 p.m. to debrief about the experience. I reluctantly agreed.

After a short workout and a long visit to the steam room to rid myself of two weeks of dirt, I headed to the lobby to wait for Fabby. I was hoping he wouldn't show up with a prostitute as a way of saying thanks. After 30 minutes of waiting, it was clear that Fabby blew off our meeting (and did not send a prostitute in his place).

Relationships Are More Valuable Than Money

Main goal of the day: Do NOT leave the orphanage with a kid.

On my last day in the Pearl of Africa, I had another first—a visit to an orphanage. The orphanage was operated by the pastor who was the subject of the book written by the wife of my South Carolina friends I met while on safari.

It took about 30 minutes to get to the orphanage. The "campus" consisted of several buildings in various stages of construction. Apparently, as funds are donated, buildings are worked on until the funds run out.

As I got out of the car, about 100 beautiful kids between the ages of 4 and 15 dressed in bright red uniforms came running towards where I was standing and surrounded me. They hugged my arms and sang beautifully. They were so happy to see me, each with a beautiful smile. Their pure joy overwhelmed me, and it was breathtaking. Words cannot describe what I felt. I was blessed to be in their presence. One song in particular was of their gratitude for being alive and living at the orphanage. Tears filled my eyes as they sang. After a tour of the facilities (the living arrangements, kitchen and classrooms), the kids put on a concert for me in a half completed room. The songs were amazing. The entire staff could not have been more welcoming and loving towards me. I will forever treasure that moment, and those children will always have a place in my heart.

The orphanage.

On the way back to my hotel, the pastor spoke to me about establishing relationships with others as a way to run a successful business. He lived by this mantra in creating, maintaining and expanding his orphanage. He may be on to something with this business model.

That entire morning left me in a state of pure joy. I was amazed at the strength, gratitude and courage of these children and just how much they enjoyed life and being alive. Simply amazing! This experience made me realize a simple smile, followed by a laugh, brings enormous joy to the world.

Kids from the orphanage.

REFLECTIVE MOMENT: Big Law could borrow the pastor's wisdom and deepen already great relationships with clients. Deepening client relationships with an SA "with pleasure" service style will lead to more meaningful client relations and expanded business opportunities.

Leaving Uganda

My trip to Uganda, the Pearl of Africa, made me think and realize the following:

1. Always change hotels if the first one is not working.

2. Always listen to the advice given by CDC workers.

3. Praying for others is an awesome way to fall asleep, especially while at 14,000 feet, hungry and freezing cold.

4. I love my kids more than ever.

5. Everyone has an agenda, especially mission people in Uganda.

6. The sights were amazing, from trekking in the Mountains of the Moon to the chimps and the mountain gorillas. Plus seeing the Big Five (lion, cape buffalo, leopard, elephant and rhinoceros) and the orphanage made this three-week part of the Adventure awesome.

7. This Adventure was no more and no less than an adult time-out. It was NOT about God, finding myself or the like. I was taking a time-out to chill, explore, smile and become a 21st Century Adventurer.

8. Even in Uganda, the TSA is a mess.

There are two primary choices in life: to accept conditions as they exist, or accept the responsibility for changing them.

—Denis Waitley

CHAPTER ELEVEN

JAMBO!

When I stepped off the plane in Tanzania, all I could think about was whether I was fit enough to make the climb to Kili's summit. I felt strong, but I knew from prior climbs that mountains like Kili are very difficult. Plus, I was expecting Kili to be more physically challenging than the Rwenzoris, and that climb pushed my physical fitness to the limit.

After I had arrived at the hotel in Arusha, our base for the climb, I asked about Mass for the next day. Without hesitation, Salvatore, a busboy (and what I later would learn, a guide for our team on the mountain) volunteered to take me. And Mass was inspirational.

The priest spoke little English throughout the Mass, but one thing he mentioned was whether we knew where our treasure was. This stuck with me and had me wondering where my treasure was? So much of my energy and time was dedicated to work, and that was my primary focus, but now, at this stage of my life, I questioned whether this focus was worth it. I was returning to my career, but I was also committed to not make my career look like the past. I was excited to create a new future and wanted my future to be about becoming a modern day adventurer with an exceptional career. And that is what happened.

A REFLECTIVE MOMENT: An adult time-out will be a foundation of a new experience. It will be the most refreshing thing a lawyer can ever do in life. It was for me. Experiencing an adult time-out is much more exhilarating than landing a new client or project and even an enormous paycheck. Taking an adult time-out will lead to a career of experiencing the pure joy and excitement of waking up each day and walking into the unknown instead of the repetitive behavior of putting on a suit, driving the same roads to the same office and then sitting behind the same desk working on the same old, same old with a mug of Starbucks in hand.

In an African Mass, at the time of the giving of gifts, rather than traditionally passing a basket from pew to pew, everyone walks to the altar to contribute. The Mass had the typical two collections, but this Mass had a third. I had no idea what the second or even third collection was for, but I partook in each offertory. When the third offertory was announced, I became aware of a boy around eight years old sitting in the same pew as me. He was alone, no parental figure with him, and was not wearing any shoes. I motioned for him to join me in walking to the front for the offering. I gave him US dollars to put in the basket. I had never seen a smile as big as his as we walked to the front of the church. He walked like he was a king. He slowly placed the cash in the basket with such pride and joy, and to my amazement, his smile grew bigger. He then paused and looked over the parishioners. Time stood still as the entire church quietly watched him. The priest smiled in delight. It was a sight to see and a very moving experience. Following the collection, the priest told the church that the third collection, which is gathered only once a month, was to raise funds for a new speaker system. He also mentioned his gratitude to the American for his generous contributions. The entire church had a good laugh.

Following Mass, I spoke with the young boy and was incredibly moved by our conversation. He lived in an orphanage near the church and regularly attended Sunday Mass. He was very curious about sports in the US, especially soccer. He just wanted to talk and was a true joy to be around.

I sought out the young priest to thank him for Mass and to ask for a blessing for a safe climb. I told him I was a bit nervous, but he assured me that God and all the angels and saints would keep me safe. I definitely felt better after receiving the blessing. He also cracked a smile while thanking me again for my contribution towards a new speaker system.

Following Mass, I had emails from all three of my kids wishing me well. Getting these emails made checking Outlook on a Sunday morning worthwhile. It put a smile on my face and warmed my heart to know they were thinking of me.

Either Way, You Are Right

Typically, RMI (the guide service for my climb) would take climbers on a tour of the local attractions prior to the scheduled climb. There was a bombing in Arusha a month earlier, and all US Embassies were ordered closed, so RMI canceled all organized trips into the city. However, Bruce, our RMI guide, said that I was free to explore the city on my own. I was open for some exploration (plus I received a blessing of protection from the priest the day before), so I hired a cab and took off for the city.

Arusha is described in the guidebooks as a fast growing seat in East Africa. Although, it was not much of a tourist destination. It is a city of approximately 300,000 people and of total and complete congestion. Clearly, the only people who come through town are on their way for a Kili climb. The "tourist" spots were not worth stopping for. It made Kampala and Maputo look cosmopolitan. I could not get back to the sanctuary of the hotel quick enough.

Waiting Around to Start the Climb

I arrived two days before the rest of my climbing team, and this gave me the opportunity to visit with several climbers who recently finished their Kili climb. They seemed to be in good spirits and not beat up physically or mentally. Some even had that post-summit high going on. It was good to talk with these climbers, but my anxiety level began to rise with each conversation. Anxiety level notwithstanding, I really enjoy climbing. I was not sure why I do extreme sports, but I have given up on understanding the "whys" of my life. It never seemed to lead to a rational explanation of why I do the things I do.

Gear Check and Team Meeting

On the morning before our first day on the mountain, we had a team meeting followed by a gear check. Knowing the painstaking time involved in an RMI gear check, I volunteered to go first and was finished in 30 minutes and in a good mood.

RMI provided a nice book illustrating each day of the climb so we knew exactly what each day would look like in terms of time on feet and altitude to be climbed. While reading the book, it hit me that climbing over 4,000 feet each day would be physically challenging. I began to have doubts, but doubts notwithstanding, my goal was to see the Roof of Africa. My determination to summit seemed to overcome, or more likely, block out, the self-doubt I was experiencing.

At our team meeting, Bruce mentioned there are four types of fun:

1. Fun like downhill skiing in powder snow.

2. Fun like mountain climbing where the memory/finish is more fun than the actual climb.

3. A mountain climber who gets sick and turns into a complainer.

4. The people who make fun of #3 when they refuse to gut it out.

Bruce made it a point that we will all experience the first part of #3, but we just needed to keep climbing and things will work out, or we will become *that climber* in everyone's memory. These rules have a kernel of truth that can be applied to all aspects of life. It reminded me that when things go bad, keep moving and eventually things will get better. Expecting a bad to remain permanent is an illusion. A bad will pass similar to a difficult part of a mountain.

A little bit about the team:

Bruce, our RMI Guide: A super nice guy who summited Mount Everest three times. He had just finished a guide on Kili and was to climb Mount Elbrus in Russia (the tallest peak in Europe) once our climb was completed. He had been with RMI for 15 years. Prior to RMI, he worked a normal corporate job until he decided to trade the suits in for sleeping bags, crampons, tents and some altitude. He loved his job.

The CA family: Julie, a dentist from Santa Monica, was with her kids who were approximately 25, 20 and 18 years old. Her oldest recently graduated college and was working in corporate America. Her middle child was a junior at the University of Oregon, and the youngest was a freshman in college in CA. It was nice to see how much the family really enjoyed being together.

Kurt and Kim: This couple was from Sun Valley, Idaho, and were in their mid-60s. They were avid cross country skiers and in excellent shape. They were mostly retired and had worked a variety of jobs over the years, including running a family golf course. Kim had unusually unique hobbies such as taxidermy, hunting (like on horses way deep in the mountains) and welding. Kim was always in good spirits.

Peter and Paula: This couple was also from Sun Valley and friends with Kurt and Kim. They quit their jobs in Alaska when they were in their early 50s and were retired. They did not have children and were active skiers. Peter had summited Mount Rainier and Mount McKinley (Denali) in the past. Peter was 71 and Paula was 68. I would never have guessed their ages, especially Peter's. It was additional proof that being an adventurous soul will keep one young in body and mind.

And then there's me:

The "look" after taking an adult time-out.

A last minute addition to our Kili climb was a single woman from Oregon. RMI was not prepared and did not have an extra tent for her. I volunteered to share mine and she was game. She was cute, athletic and definitely a novice climber. She brought more altitude sickness pills than anyone could imagine having, but I really liked her spirited nature.

Like any great adventure, romance always transpires (or at least we hope it does). My Adventure copied that script. Tempting to describe our mountain romance in detail, I will embrace the gentleman's approach to a "no kiss and tell" policy and let your imagination run wild with what romance looks like on a 19,000-plus foot mountain, in a small tent and breathing hard (because oxygen was lacking, of course).

The Climb

The Climb: Day 1
   Machame Gate (5,900 ft./ 1,798 m.) to Machame Camp (9,890 ft./ 3,014 m.)
   Vertical Change: +3,990 ft.(1,216 m.)
   Distance: 6 miles (9.7 km.)
   Average Temperatures: 45°–60°F (7°–16°C)

   RMI Notes for the Day: We travel to the Kilimanjaro National Park Entrance at the Machame Gate. After registering with the park, we begin the climb. Leaving the cultivation zone, where bananas and coffee plants abound, we travel into the forest zone, the lush rainforest of Kilimanjaro's lower slopes. The trail begins as an old Jeep road before turning into a narrow but well-traveled path climbing through the jungle. The trail winds through thick vegetation and enormous trees. Keep an eye out for the occasional blue or colobus monkeys that can be spotted in the canopy above. Approaching camp, we enter the giant heather of the heather and moorland zone. Some of this heather can grow to over 30 ft.(9 m.) tall.

It was show time and I was ready. We began our first day with a 45-minute truck ride to the entrance of the mountain. I was both nervous and excited. All I could think of was my desire to make it up *and* back down. It would be my first of the Seven Summits, I hoped.

The day's climb turned out to be simple, straightforward and not very demanding. We had some light rain but nothing too difficult for me to handle. My previous climbs have taught me that steepness and difficulties were not far away so I couldn't help fearing that "diffi-

cult" was only a day away. The unknown of the next day produced unwanted anxiety and made falling asleep on the rocky and cold ground difficult. I'd like to think my evening prayers of asking the angels and saints to protect me from anxiety helped.

Camping on the way to the Roof.

The Climb: Day 2
Machame Camp (9,890 ft./ 3,014 m.) to Shira Camp (12,570 ft./ 3,831 m.)
Vertical Change: +2,680 ft.(817 m.) / -150 ft.(46 m.)
Distance: 2.75 miles (4.4 km.)
Average Temperatures: 40°–55°F (4°–13°C)

Notes for the Day: The trail becomes steeper and rockier as the vegetation thins and we leave the giant heather. There are several rock bands a few feet high that we must climb over. Gradually the gnarled trunks of the giant heather disappear, and we enter the moorland, grasses and rocky terrain unique to Eastern Africa. It is common to see wildflowers, giant lobelias and senecios in this area. After ascending a wide ridge, we gain the broad and sloping Shira Plateau. We descend a few hundred feet along the edge of the Shira Plateau into our camp tucked among the sparse vegetation and volcanic rock bands. On a clear evening, Shira Camp offers beautiful views of Kilimanjaro's upper stretches as well as of Mount Meru and the town of Arusha.

Day two's climb was a four-and-a-half hour very manageable trek. I trekked behind Bruce most of the day, and it felt good to keep pace with an experienced guide. Bruce became more and more open with us about his life and his experiences. Hilarious stories were told about previous clients who were crazy, climbers acting as six-year-olds when things went wrong and how altitude can even make one poop in their pants. But stories of complainers, although seriously funny, cautioned me to avoid becoming a future story for a mountain guide.

The Climb: Day 3
Shira Camp (12,570 ft./ 3,831 m.) to Barranco Camp (13,030 ft./ 3,972 m.)
Vertical Change: +2,280 ft.(695 m.) / -1,820 ft.(555 m.)
Distance: 5.75 miles (9.3 km.)
Average Temperatures: 30°–45°F (-1°–7°C)

Notes for the Day: Large volcanic boulders dot the landscape as we enter the dry and rocky terrain of the highland desert zone. We climb directly toward the summit crater of Kilimanjaro, known as Kibo. The trail gently ascends the Shira Plateau until we reach our high point near Lava Tower at 14,900 ft.(4,542 m.). Above us hang the glaciers of the steep Southern Breach Wall, the south face of Kibo. The descent into the Barranco Valley begins steeply but soon levels out as we reach the valley floor and follow it to camp. Keep an eye out for caves carved into the volcanic cliffs above the valley. Near the Barranco Camp, reenter the upper portion of the heather and moorland zone where many of the mountain's most impressive giant groundsels can be found. We make camp near these bizarre flowering plants that grow up to 30 feet tall.

Day three turned into a six-hour demanding and heart-pounding trek. It was much more challenging than the previous two days combined. My heart raced and my breathing became difficult. The elevation could be felt by all of us, and I could sense that cold and challenging trekking was now upon us.

I hung out after each day's climb with Bruce in the dining tent drinking tea. Listening to stories of other climbers and the crazy things people do at elevation brought tears to our faces. The laughter among us was just too much. The two couples from Idaho joined us one night, and it was equally fun, hanging with people and talking about nothing in particular was memorable.

During the day I also had great conversations with the local guides while trekking. They taught me the local saying "poli poli" which translates into "go slow." It was a reminder that I no longer had to put my head down and plow through the game of life.

Eric was one of my favorite local guides. He would come up to me while trekking singing "Hakuna Matata" from the *Lion King*. We didn't know all the lyrics, but we did get the "no worries for the rest of your days" part right. Singing at 15,000 feet was awesome. I think I may have actually carried a tune.

The Climb: Day 4
Barranco Camp (13,030 ft./ 3,972 m.) to Karanga Camp (13,160 ft./ 4,011 m.)
Vertical Change: +1,040 ft.(317 m.) / -940 ft.(287 m.)
Distance: 2.5 miles (4.4 km.)
Average Temperatures: 30°–45°F (-1°–7°C)

Notes for the Day: We climb the Barranco Wall right out of the camp. The steep ascent traverses a series of ledges up the face, climbing up several rock bands that require you to use your hands to ascend. After reaching the top of the Barranco Wall, we traverse between 13,000 ft. (3,962 m.) and 14,500 ft.(4,420 m.) on a rocky trail, climbing in and out of several valleys that drain the summit massif. The impressive southern side of Kilimanjaro, capped by the Diamond, Balletto, Heim, Kersten and Decken Glaciers, hangs above us. In the valley floors we find small streams and pockets of blooming lobelias and flowers bordering the small streams. A short climb out of the Karanga Valley leads directly into camp.

We finally made it to our first serious and difficult portion of the climb: the Barranco Wall. And difficult it was. The climb was one-and-a-half hours straight up the face of the mountain.

As I forced breakfast down, staring at the Wall, I could see the headlights of climbers scattered at various sections, and it was very intimidating. As we began the climb, we kept saying *poli poli* and slowly made the ascent, step by step. There were two spots where one could actually fall off the mountain. We had experienced guides who would inform us when to "kiss" the rocks so as to lean into the side for balance and luckily, no one in my group fell backward. It was an intense, and thrilling, portion of the climb. After reaching the top of the Wall, we had a well-deserved break before an easy two-hour trek to our next camp.

A REFLECTIVE MOMENT: I realized I did not need to change the Firm or even the Tax Department to move my ERISA practice into the zone of genius; I simply need a new service delivery model for clients. The challenge, however, will be to stay within a zone of genius and resist being sucked into the petty minutia that occupies so many conversations in the hallways, break rooms and worse, over dinner and drinks with disgruntled lawyers.

The Climb: Day 5
Karanga Camp (13,160 ft./ 4,011 m.) to Barafu Camp (15,200 ft./ 4,633 m.)
Vertical Change: +2,040 ft.(622 m.)
Distance: 2 miles (3.2 km.)
Average Temperatures: 30°–40°F (-1°–7°C)

Notes for the Day: We leave the last of the vegetation and climb through the rocky volcanic terrain to our high camp, which is perched on a ridge running down from the southeast edge of Kilimanjaro's summit. While the trail weaves through the rocky volcanic terrain, our travel is straight forward. Impressive views of the surrounding plateaus that fall away into the jungles below give perspective to the scale of Kilimanjaro's geography.

Following a short three-hour manageable trek, we arrived at "high camp." High camp was at approximately 15,000 feet and was our launching point for the summit. At this point, the possibility of reaching the summit was turning into a reality, and I became excited. Our plans were to eat an early dinner, hit the sleeping bags and try to sleep. We would wake around 11 p.m. for a small, quick meal and then start the climb at midnight and hopefully reach the summit by 7 a.m., just in time to watch the sunrise. There was a nervous excitement in the air as we mulled around camp. I reminded myself constantly of rule number one of mountaineering: going up is optional and down mandatory. I was ready and confident about the task at hand as I got into my sleeping bag for a quick nap on top of some cold, lumpy rocks.

In Life, Keep Climbing

The team was ready. Bruce was well organized and felt good about everyone's ability. Bruce, however, made it clear that the team will not slow if a climber had to stop. This is the harsh reality of mountain climbing. Climbers climb, and if you can't make it, the other climbers still climb. I was determined to be with the latter group of climbers.

A REFLECTIVE MOMENT: Solo adventures bring out a deep appreciation for loved ones. This was a great surprise for me.

The Roof of Africa!

The Climb: Day 6
   Barafu Camp (15,200 ft./ 4,633 m.) to Summit (19,340 ft./ 5,895 m.) to Mweka (10,080 ft./ 3,292 m.)
   Vertical Change: +4,140 ft.(1,262 m.) / -9,260 ft.(2,822 m.)
   Distance: Barafu to Summit is 2.5 miles (4 km.) Summit to Mweka is 7 miles (11.2 km.)
   Average Temperatures: 15°–25°F (-9°–4°C)
   Notes for the Day: SUMMIT DAY! Making a pre-dawn start, we climb through the night ascending Kilimanjaro's upper slopes and enter the summit zone. We follow the switchbacked trail up soft volcanic soil, climbing along the side of Rebmann Glacier until we reach Stella Point on the crater rim. We follow the crater rim, walking between the towering ice walls of Kilimanjaro's Southern Icefield on our left and overlooking

the massive volcanic crater on our right, to Kilimanjaro's summit, Uhuru
Peak. On the descent, we continue through Barafu Camp to Mweka
Camp at 10,080 ft.(3,292 m.), passing from Kilimanjaro's summit
zone all the way back into the giant heather and moorland zone.

I made it to the Roof of Africa!

Standing on the Roof of Africa was an amazing accomplishment.
Climbing with headlights for six hours over and around massive boulders made for an exhausting climb. With every step I took, I needed
to pause to take a breath. We would climb for an hour in light coats
and then put on heavy down parkas as we rested for ten minutes to
hydrate and eat a small snack. The last two hours of the climb was
not only difficult but freezing cold. In fact, my two water bottles were
completely frozen by the time we reached the summit. My team moved
quickly, and we were able to reach the summit just in time for sunrise.
At such a height, the view was simply breathtaking. I could see for

miles as Africa woke for the day. I experienced a high not even the backpackers from Port St. Johns could achieve. As I rested at 19,340 feet, sitting on a cold rock overlooking Africa, listening to the silence that surrounded me, I became emotional. Tears of joy were rolling down my frozen face. I wished my family was with me to share in this tremendous accomplishment.

Trivializing a Kili climb as merely a hike along a well-worn trail is misguided. Bruce mentioned that many people downplay the significance of a Kili climb. He refers to them as the "voice of the non-participant." He said that until you've climbed Kili, your voice does not count. You are a non-participating voice in someone else's incredible achievement. Many people have failed to summit Kili, including professional athletes—just ask the mighty Ray Lewis or Martina Navratilova about their *attempt* to summit.

After an hour soaking in an incredible atmosphere, we began trekking down to 10,000 feet, the altitude for our camp that night. My goal was to embrace the s*low is smooth and smooth is fast* as well as the *poli poli* mantra on the descent. I am just plain slow on all descents, but I made it down in seven hours and felt good along the way. By the time I hit camp, I was ready for some food (calories) and bed. It was a full 14-hour day, and I was outright beat. At dinner that last night, the conversations shifted to having some beers and a three-day safari. We were all ready to be out of sleeping bags and into clean clothes after a long, hot shower.

A REFLECTIVE MOMENT: Trekking down from the Roof of Africa will make one realize that lawyers must live life according to one's wants and not the wants of others. I committed, with each step, to start acting a bit selfish.

On the way down from the summit, I trekked for an hour or so with Stan. Stan was a typical Tanzanian guide, approximately 30 years old with a young child or two and who had school tuition he was hoping I would fit the bill for (or at least contribute towards). Even Salvatore, who took me to Mass twice and was always ready

Eric, my favorite local Kili guide.

to help out with whatever I needed, broke out with the, "I need cash for my children's education." He even handed me paperwork with wiring instructions. Yes, wiring instructions for $3,000. I believe he needed help to defray the cost of school tuition, but I'm not sure school costs that much in Tanzania.

Stan referred to himself as "Easy Peasy Lemon Squeezy." Where he learned this phrase and from whom I had no idea, but he was a super nice guy. It was clear this was not his first rodeo with Americans on a high priced trek up a mountain. It seemed all guides would say the right things and compliment each of us for being "strong as lions." Now, I knew they were full of it. But overall, I could not have asked for a better group of local guides, even if they wanted extra money for school tuition.

The Climb: Day 7
Mweka Camp (10,080 ft./ 3,292 m.) to Mweka Gate (6,000 ft./ 1,829 m.)
Vertical Change: -4,080 ft.(1,244 m.)
Distance: 4.75 miles (7.6 km.)
Average Temperatures: 45°–60°F (7°–16°C)

Notes for the Day: We descend through the giant heather into the forest zone as we approach the end of the trail. The well-worn trail weaves through the jungle for another several thousand feet until we reach the gate. The symphony of sights, sounds and smells pleasantly overwhelms us after the days at high altitudes, and the air feels thick and warm. Keep an eye out for blue colobus monkeys and the small and colorful Kilimanjaro impatiens flowers. Upon reaching the Mweka Gate, we settle into our vehicle and make the drive back to the hotel.

When we arrived back to the hotel, the wait staff made a huge deal out of our accomplishment with a native congratulatory song while handing us glasses of wine. We all danced in the parking lot before hitting the showers. We were all on a "climber's high" and it was a great way to end the experience. At our celebratory dinner at the hotel, I bought the team a couple bottles of delicious champagne as we all relaxed and enjoyed a proper dinner. But no one stayed past dessert as a comfortable bed awaited us all.

Once we were off the intensity of the mountain, all things changed with my Oregonian bunk mate. As with the tent situation, RMI was not able to arrange a separate room for her on our safari. Being a true Texan gentleman, I offered that she share my room. I figured the worst thing that could happen was she would say no thanks and leave Tanzania early. But my charisma and charm led to a fun final four days of my Kili adventure. It had been some time since I stayed up late and woke up early just talking about nothing in particular with a woman who was clearly beyond college theatrics. Having conversations about work, adventurous travel, family and life in general brought a smile to my face.

Never Stop Making Your Own Decisions

We were up early the next morning for our safari. We were excited to be off the mountain, in clean clothes and not having to trek. On the way out of town, we stopped at a grocery store for some beer to drink while on safari. It was great sipping on a cold beer observing wildlife, most of which I had already seen in Uganda. I had seen enough monkeys to last a lifetime. But clearly the safari took second fiddle to being off the mountain and drinking a cold beer.

Refreshments following summit day.

Our first lodge, the Plantation Lodge, was incredible. The rooms, common areas, dining room and the grounds were all first class. Similar to Uganda, this place had guards with AK-47s to keep animals out. After checking out the lodge, Bruce, my Oregon friend and I had some SA wine on a patio. This was the bottle I purchased in Stellenbosch

from the winery that specialized in Pinotage (and I carried it with
me for what seemed like forever). It was nice to sit outside, drink
delicious wine and gaze at some phenomenal hotel grounds with lots
of guests walking around. The atmosphere was very festive for being
in the middle of Tanzania.

The Quiet of the Morning

I continued my morning ritual of coffee
while sitting at a table and writing. My
morning coffee had become a special
moment of the day for me. Mornings were
serene and peaceful, and I really came to
appreciate the quiet and solitude of them,
Oregon friend notwithstanding.

On safari.

A REFLECTIVE MOMENT: If only everyone knew it was an
illusion that one cannot take an adult time-out from a successful
career. Taking time off in the middle of a career is an absolute no
brainer. Period. My entire Firm became more profitable on account
of my time-out.[4]

Another Safari Day

My last safari day was billed as a day of watching lions, elephants and
giraffes. But I had had my fill of wild animals by then. That safari day
was one day too long for me.

But sitting in a truck did give me time to think about my African
experience. Africa was amazing on many levels. From my first stop in
Cape Town, to the safari post-Kili, my eyes opened to a world I never
knew truly existed. Interacting with the locals profoundly changed my

---

4 In the 12 months following my return to Big Law, my revenues increased
dramatically. I attribute this to being 100 percent different within the confines
of the 47th floor. In addition, not a single client left during my Adventure
and, in fact, many engaged me in projects that historically the ERISA group
was not retained to do.

perspective of this entire continent. Africans are hard workers who want change and prosperity. I hope their beautiful land is not taken over by the Hiltons and Marriotts of the world. I now understand China's interest in Africa.

On safari.

Although experiencing this side of the world had been amazing, I was looking forward to Italy. I was ready for some western style comfort, normal roads and a nice comfortable bed. Sleeping in thin tents was getting a little too old. I was also ready for the final act of my Adventure—the marathon.

Explore the World

On my last night in Africa, I woke suddenly with a loud and clear thought on my mind: *explore the world*. It was a strong pestering feeling, and I began to wonder why this was harassing my mind. It then hit me. I needed to incorporate *explore the world* into my way of life, not only for the remainder of my Adventure, but in all aspects of my life going forward.

CHAPTER TWELVE

OUT OF AFRICA

Africa was an enlightening experience. It had an impact on how I viewed the world, life and work. As I boarded the plane headed for Italy, I couldn't help but think that all was good in my life. As for my Oregon friend, we said our goodbyes at the Arusha Airport. It was fun getting to know her, and we had some good laughs on how our sleeping accommodations came to be.

Big Adventures Don't Fit in the Overhead

People began asking me what the punch line to my Adventure was. Besides getting closer to the end, it had me thinking long and hard about what the heck I'd done with my life over the last four months. I had unplugged from the Big Law machine, decided that Big Law was not for me and that I would never return. Then I had an epiphany, a realization that I can incorporate a different style of working within the confines of a career in Big Law, a way where I can include my wants and desires in my work life. I know what Big Law wants, unspoken or not, and I needed to incorporate their needs with *my* needs. I didn't want to get to the end of my life with regret and wish I had done things differently. I was adamant and confident that I would not perpetuate my past.

A REFLECTIVE MOMENT: While on the plane to Rome, the plane's monitor reflected all the countries I would like to visit. The places and people that one misses by taking an airplane was staring me in the face. This was exactly Nicholas' point on why he takes trains, buses and ships as his mode of transportation.

I also began to look forward to my next phase of "Mark" being the person that God created me to be. I was committed to avoiding the trap of my old winning formula at work, keeping my head down, billing hours and otherwise continuing the insanity of my past. I had to become more than just a billing machine delivering exceptional legal work. After all, I had evolved into the most interesting ERISA modern day adventurer.

The Clint Eastwood movie *Trouble with the Curve* was playing on the plane. Here was a guy (Clint) facing the end of his career, a young executive who thought he knew what was right (and wanted Clint fired), a daughter who was pissed about how Clint raised her and Clint doing his own thing the way he wanted in the face of these challenges. It had me thinking of my challenges when I was faced with societal and Firm expectations of how to live and perform, and the following thoughts came to mind:

1. People do not know the struggles and sacrifices I had to make in order to get to where I am today.

2. I had lived and performed work according to a dysfunctional sense of responsibility in all areas of my life.

3. The Firm may want something from me that I no longer can give. I, however, no longer can live according to its implicative code. I was now free from the imaginary chains of a primitive work system.

4. I had integrated selfishness as a way to live my future. If people cannot accept my way of being, it is now their problem.

5. I am completely comfortable with pursuing my wants. I can no longer expect others to guess what they are anymore. Only I can create the change I need when faced with challenges.

CHAPTER THIRTEEN

A WALKABOUT ROME

The Roman Colosseum.

My first day began at the Vatican. I climbed to the top of St. Peter's, hung out at the church and said some prayers of thanks for a safe journey. Then, I was off to explore one of my favorite cities. It was an awesome walkabout that included a stop at my Firm's Rome office for a few hours. While sitting in a conference room, I experienced a different level of energy being at the "office." It actually put a smile on my face. A smile that had been lacking for many years.

A REFLECTIVE MOMENT: I was having coffee with someone in Rome who mentioned that trips similar to my Adventure are usually instigated by a personal tragedy. My Gap Period was anything but that. I simply needed to S-T-O-P, hit the refresh button and act outside the norm of the expectations of a lawyer in Big Law. Somewhere along the way of bill, bill and bill, I lost the love of my career. I needed to reclaim my adventurous soul. I was not happy with who I had evolved into and where I was heading. I truly believe all progress is made outside the box of tradition, and in making my Adventure happen, I went way outside that traditional box and rediscovered a career.

Why Tropea?

Beach life.

After two nights in Rome, I was off to a southern Italian beach destination, Tropea. I first visited Tropea several years earlier to take an immersion class to perfect my Italian. The village was located on the

Mediterranean Sea and was spectacular. The exquisite beach, town square and cafés could not be beaten, and Americans were nowhere to be found. The six-hour trip from Rome with a bottle of wine and some cheese made for a delicious lunch that I shared with a couple seated next to me who tolerated my broken Italian. It turned out to be a super enjoyable train ride.

While the train was heading south, I received an email from the head of my Firm's New York office asking me to commit to working in NYC two weeks per month upon my return. This was an incredible opportunity to build and expand our ERISA practice in NYC. I knew I could deliver what was expected, and this fed my adventurous soul. I felt the universe was shining a light on my return to my career.[5]

A Time for Integration

On the morning of my first day in Tropea, I took a brisk run around town, had breakfast and took a nap on the beach all before noon. I was convinced after my run that I was prepared for the upcoming marathon. I was in great shape, especially after my climbs of the Rwenzoris and Kili.

As I relaxed on the beach, I couldn't help but go back into a work-thinking mindset. I was ready to integrate a sense of curiosity and adventure into a career and create a new functional work relationship with others. I had no idea how I would assimilate this, but I knew I could not have the same thoughts, responses, actions, reactions and the like to the same issues I was presented with each day in the practice of Big Law. I reminded myself that sometimes Big Law can be difficult, challenging and stressful (and this is not always a bad thing). Although I was determined to create a new experience come

---

5 As it turned out, I rented an apartment in Chelsea and just completed my third year of working in New York every other week. Time spent in New York has been fantastic. I have yet to have a bad day. My client base has exploded and I am now in service to an entirely new client base. Based in part on my success, the Firm has encouraged other Texas lawyers to consider making a similar move to NYC. Cross selling NYC with Texas has been and will continue to be a benefit to clients.

September, the early morning emails regarding various issues and projects that flowed into my BlackBerry were not going to deter me from making the final days of my Gap Period extraordinary.

The Mountains

I took a break from beach life for a few days, drove to the mountains of Aspromonte and then around the toe of Italy.

The Aspromonte region is located at the very tip of the toe. The region offers a unique opportunity to stand on a beach or on a ski slope within the same hour. The mountains are probably best known, though, as the home of Ndrangheta, the Calabrian mafia.

Going into mountains, by car or foot, immediately shifts my mood, perspective and outlook—all for the best. It was a beautiful drive to the mountains. It was slow and smooth, notwithstanding getting pulled over by the local police for going too slow and generally not knowing where I was going. The officer that pulled me over was curious as to where I was going and more curiously, why. He got a chuckle out of my broken Italian but gave me directions and wished me well.

Aim High,
Time Flies

The first mountain town I stayed in was quiet as dust until midnight when all hell broke loose. The locals descended on the streets as if they had just been let out of a Midnight Mass, with loud noises and music playing everywhere. From my hotel balcony, I watched all the festivities for an hour or so, but they continued well into the night. It was a strange town to visit for sure. No tourists and not one person spoke English.

The following day, I headed to the national park for some hiking—a nice change of pace from the beach scene. While hiking, I came across several old men digging for truffles (*trifolau*—meaning truffle diggers) on the side of the mountains. As I came to learn, truffle digging is a very big and serious business in Italy. The trifolaus are very secretive regarding their locations and most dig at night to hide from other trifolaus. They use trained truffle-sniffing dogs to find their locations.

They are not just selling it locally but throughout all of Italy, especially at truffle festivals which are held in Italy every year. They generally sell for 600 to 1,300 euros depending on their size/weight.

I stopped at a small coffee shop for a cappuccino after the hike. The proprietor was a middle aged woman who was trying desperately to have me hire her adult son to guide me up the side of the mountain. The son looked like a city slicker from NYC and not much of a mountain climber. Not sure what he was doing in the park in the middle of the day in dress pants and dress shoes, but I politely declined his guide services and drove off to explore some other mountain cities.

Be kind, for everyone you meet is fighting a battle you know nothing about.
—Wendy Mass, *The Candymakers*

I had lunch in the mountain town of Gambiere, which was more of a winter skiing town than a summer destination. The city center was active with people out and about, and I decided to stay for the next two nights (instead of staying in my last hotel). As I checked out of my hotel from the night before, a group of 30 men gathered in the alley next to the hotel. They were surrounded by a dozen huge, brightly colored funeral wreaths. The men were mulling around with hands in pockets and black coats zipped to the neckline. No one spoke a word. There were no women nor any children present. It looked very mafia-like. As I was packing the car, everyone just stared at me. It was spooky scary—like *Godfather* scary. It was good that I was leaving.

My Mom's Birthday

I went on some amazing trails, including climbing the tallest mountain peak in the range. The views of Sicilia, the never ending coastline and ships navigating the waters were incredible. It reminded me of when the container ship made its way past Sicilia. On the drive down from the mountain, I stopped and asked a group of hikers for directions to a trail I wasn't able to locate. It turned out they were actually an extended family out for an afternoon trek and a picnic. After driving for a while, I stopped again for another quick hike, and lo and behold, there was that same family enjoying their lunch—*and boy was it a lunch*. The entire picnic table was covered with food, beer, wine and espresso. They insisted I stay and eat with them. Insisted was an understatement—they were adamant, Italian style with arms flying every which way. Only one of the kids spoke broken English, and to my surprise, my Italian had improved. We talked about Disney World and New York City, places they dreamed of visiting someday. I was more curious about the mafia. Somehow, even with my below average Italian, we all managed to have good laughs, and best of all, lunch was great. I had a huge salami and cheese sandwich, a beer and an espresso. They even packed me a to go bag for dinner. They were such a generous family and full of laughter even though I was not too sure what they were talking about at times.

My Italian friends.

A REFLECTIVE MOMENT: Nothing can replace the love of family. Looking for a replacement to what a family brings to one's soul only leads to disappointment and a lonely existence. The Italian family made me think of my own, particularly my mom. It was her birthday, and I was miles away from her. Not a moment went by that I didn't think of her and wished she was with me enjoying this incredible spread. That day, I really appreciated her devotion to her family. She lives an incredible and inspirational life. She has attained a level of peace in this world unmatched by any other, and I can only hope that her way of being rubs off on me. Maybe daily Mass, lots of prayers and a glass of white wine at dinner are the secret ingredients to attaining this level of peace.

My New Friends

As my Adventure wound down, I thought about all of the interesting people I met along the way. People I never would have encountered had I stayed working back on the 47th floor drafting pension plans. People like:

1. The freighter captain and his excitement over his Victoria's Secret purchases;

2. The Ukrainian officers, especially the two electricians, one of whom also acted as the ship's barber;

3. The ship's cook and the guitar playing and singing we did after dinner;

4. Nicholas, my shipmate on the CMA CGM Jamaica;

5. The yoga instructors in Cape Town;

6. The bar scene at the Whisky Bar, especially the guy washing the lady's feet with expensive champagne;

7. The hotel staff in SA (Jamestown, Plettenberg Bay, Durban, Port St. Johns, Jeffrey's Bay, the Marine Hotel) with their "with pleasure" service;

8. The police in SA and my attempt to get arrested;

9. My time with the backpackers sitting around a fire pit, canoeing in the mountains and enjoying their secondhand smoke;

10. Fantaman and his broken wheels;

11. My night with a Ugandan prostitute and how she exhausted me;

12. The orphanage with their lovely voices;

13. The newlyweds and the wedding party;

14. The group that traveled with me to the Roof of Africa; and finally

15. The Italian family and the importance of family gatherings.

These people will stay with me for my lifetime (Facebook will also help).

Becoming Selfish

Please make sure that you secure your oxygen mask before helping others.
—United Airlines

I typically don't believe in having "aha" moments, but my Adventure had proved otherwise. I came to realize (and appreciate) that my Adventure was more than a collection of memories of people I met and places I've visited. The Adventure produced many different emotions and many aha moments. The journey from leaving Big Law to returning with a new purpose to incorporating *explore the world* within my daily work, all left me curious as to how my future would unfold. But my biggest single aha moment was realizing that I needed to put me first, to become selfish in my life. I don't mean the selfishness that comes from the people that we try to avoid or tolerate at best. What I am promoting is a life that puts *self* before service to others.

On an airplane, you are instructed to put on your oxygen mask prior to helping others. That is the sort of selfishness that I am talking about. You must secure your own identity before you can be of service to others in an authentic manner. The heightened awareness will result in increased client service and satisfaction and will move the delivery of legal services beyond clocking billable hours to a service model of a "with pleasure" style attached.

In my world of work, I was trained to carry a BlackBerry and cell phone at all times, but most of all be available for client calls at all hours, no matter what. It was so engrained that I never thought twice about sitting in a hotel room on vacation modifying documents or participating in conference calls. Billable hours always came first no matter what. Lawyers in Big Law simply cannot divorce (or even get a separation) from their work.

Serving others at the sacrifice of "self" was draining. I now realize and believe that sacrificing a weekend of fun to finish a project, that in reality could wait, breeds only unconscious resentment. I no longer wanted to accumulate this unhealthy baggage. When a person sacrifices—resentment is only natural. I believe this to be a universal truth.

When I reflect on the missionaries I met in Uganda, I believe they were on a trip to see animals all cloaked in a spiritual and religious pretense to build a school. These missionaries were not in selfless service to others, but rather, they wanted to be selfish and see elephants in Uganda. If they were true to themselves and acknowledged they wanted to (a) go to Africa and (b) see some wildlife, then the school building they constructed would have much more meaning to all (even spiritually). Fantaman was truthful when he mentioned that everyone has an agenda beyond what you believe they are doing. My agenda is now to be selfish, and I know the direct effect of this will be a positive change in my career and the clients that I serve. Becoming the man

God intended me to be will change the world (and on a more micro level, make being a lawyer fun and meaningful).

I also no longer wanted to follow the path of every other Big Law lawyer and work to buy that next model of car and accumulate a huge 401(k) account. I was determined to blaze a trail in Big Law created by me rather than follow the worn down path of prior lawyers. For the first time in my career, I felt centered, and my path would be focused on selfless service. My oxygen mask was securely on and the oxygen was flowing (even if the bag did not inflate).

Packing Is Getting Old

As my Italian part of the Adventure was coming to an end, I realized that I was (a) so tired of cramming clothes into my backpack, (b) ready to be home and (c) *not* in marathon shape (my last few runs ended in complete exhaustion around mile ten. I think I spent too many afternoons eating gelato instead of running). This last point had me a bit concerned, but unlike Kili, where I could not simply quit, I knew the worst that could happen was that I would catch a ride to the finish line.

A Tarantella Music Festival and a Trailer Park

On my way back to Tropea, I stopped at a tiny seaside village located along a beautiful coastline with breathtaking beaches. This stretch of purely white sandy beach had many half-finished hotels and condos. The 2008 recession was still in full bloom. Believing I could find a hotel easily proved problematic. But next to the restaurant I was having lunch at was a trailer park. Yes, a trailer park. Curiously, I checked it out. It took a while to find the office, but once I did, I decided the trailer park would be "home" for the next three nights.

The trailer I rented had a single bedroom, kitchen, living room, its own bathroom and the best part—a front porch. My neighbors were what you would expect to see in a trailer park, lots of beer bellies and loud music from the 60s blasting, but it was a remarkable experience. I purchased food at a nearby grocery store and ate lunch and dinner on my porch. I had never stayed in a trailer park before, but like many things on my Adventure, I created an experience that would not have happened had I been back on the 47th floor.

I sat among the many other "parkers" eating platters of cheese and the three "W's"—wine, water and watermelon. During one dinner, I returned a call to one of my law partners, Bill. He was aware I was taking a trip but was amazed I had been gone for four months. "Miller, how did you pull the trip off," were his first words. He proceeded to tell me how he would love to do a trip like mine but, *"No way could I do that with all my clients and work responsibilities."* I wish I had a dollar for every time someone used that phrase. Bill had traveled the world while in school and understood what I was doing. He was an adventurous soul but was addicted to work (and not in a bad way). Bill was an incredible rainmaker, great with clients and co-workers and worked harder and longer than all others at the Firm. He thrived on Big Law. And Big Law rewards these types handsomely. It is a perfect marriage when it works.

Speaking with Bill made me come to appreciate my success at the Firm and most aspects of the Big Law game. At a deep level within my soul, *I wanted to want* to have the drive of a Bill. But I didn't have it. And now I realized that was okay.

On my first night I was off to the local tarantella musical festival in the city center located high on the cliffs. Tarantella is one of the most recognized forms of traditional southern Italian music with an upbeat tempo accompanied with tambourines.

The festival had a great atmosphere. It was jam-packed with all ages, young, old and in between. I did not understand what was being sung, but the vibe was electric, energetic, and the music was great. Similar to a county fair but so much cooler with lots of food, beer and wine. I also had gelato, which I now considered to be in its own food group. The festival also had many crafts for sale, including tambourines (and I bought one for my music collection).

Add "Well-Traveled" to Your Résumé

I sat among the locals, drank some wine and relaxed listening to the music which started playing around 10:30 p.m. The young kids danced, and the 20-something-year-old guys were hitting on the girls. It was a night of pure fun that lasted until 2 a.m. Once it ended, I took a stroll along the beach. Along the promenade, there were lots of cafés and people were everywhere. One café served every imaginable item covered with Nutella—it was a definite must stop. I ordered a Nutella covered waffle (since it was almost breakfast time), and it was out-of-this-world fantastic. Texas-sized stars, a tambourine and some Nutella were hard to beat that night.

The Voice of the Non-Participant

A REFLECTIVE MOMENT: Sitting on a porch, by yourself at a trailer park, will make one realize how much of the voice of the non-participant dictates what one does, who one is and who one has become. Abdicating one's voice for that of another's is not living one's life. Society as a whole will become better if we begin to reclaim the life that we are each meant to live. The voice of the non-participant should not be invited into one's own life decisions. Besides, it is none of your business what others think of you and the decisions you make.

This Is Not Your Practice Life.
This Is All There Is.

One of the many gifts of this Adventure was the new relationship with my family, particularly with my Aunt Patricia and Aunt Mary Ann. It was a complete joy to connect with them. Every email I received from them produced an instant smile, especially my Aunt Mary Ann, who followed my travels on her old hardback *World Book Encyclopedia*.

I am also very grateful for the following traveling companions: The Lord; the Virgin Mary; Saints Joseph, Jude, Anthony, Bernard, Christopher, Mark, Stephen and Sebastian and all the other saints and angels (my "Group of Friends") that protected me and kept me safe. They were such a reassuring group.

A REFLECTIVE MOMENT: It is arrogant to think that we control our future. God has the plan and the journey. It is up to us to trust and live the life we are each meant to live. With faith, you don't have to worry about your future. Faith gives one peace in whatever circumstance you're in.

This Gap Period tested my faith. I was willing to go without pay and even to the extreme of quitting. My faith guided me through the manuscript phase, kept me safe and healthy through my travels and made me wiser. Living life based on faith and without worry is truly a blessed way to live.

CHAPTER FOURTEEN

GOODBYE ITALIA—OFF TO BORDEAUX

Every year my Houston running club picks a destination marathon race, and in September 2013, Bordeaux was picked. Running a marathon in Bordeaux would be a great finale to my Adventure, I thought in the spring of 2013. How hard could it be to run 26 miles after climbing Kili?

The Marathon Expo

Pre-race day was a time of nervous excitement. Ever since high school track, I became nervous before races and aging had not cured this feeling. At the race expo, everyone seemed very fit and ready to run, except for me. I thought the only way to finish the race was to take the slow and smooth—*poli poli*—approach to the run. After the expo, I met up with my Houston running club at a pre-race dinner which turned into an all-out party. There were at least 1,000 runners eating terrible food, drinking delicious wine and listening to a third-rate band. We all danced and had a great time. Normally, one would not undertake such activities on the eve of a marathon, but it was all in good fun with lots of laughs. The night concluded with a show of spectacular fireworks.

Marathon Day

I ran my first and only marathon when I was a sophomore in high school. This time around, I realized that (a) I was not in high school anymore, (b) I was not in marathon running shape, (c) somehow my mind played a trick on me into thinking that I was and (d) it was too late to turn back when I reached mile 15 and experienced excruciating pain. Stumbling across the finish line, hoping that I would not collapse, I said to my waiting friends, "I have done many stupid things in my life, but this was the dumbest thing I have ever done." I was in severe pain with every muscle in my body hurting.

Feeling Complete

I left Bordeaux the day after my marathon and headed to Paris. My Gap Period had 24 hours left, and I was determined to make my last hours a day of pure joy, celebrate my adult time-out and embrace pulling off something that had never happened in the 100-year history of the Firm. I decontextualized what was possible within the code of the Firm. I knew, as I set out to explore Paris, that Jerry McGuire would be proud of me. I pushed the boundaries of my comfort zone (and the Firm's) and survived (as did the Firm). There were no client complications and, in fact, business exploded upon my return.[6]

I began my final day with coffee and a yogurt at the first café I spotted. I was then off to the Louvre, but an enormously long line

---

6 Within 12 months of my return I was retained by three major companies that were allegedly tied to other untouchable law firm relationships. These new relationships began so well that they effectively outsourced their entire benefits department to my group. They created ERISA work traditionally not done for the last 26 years at my Firm. The sophistication and complexity of these projects made my entire group thrilled to be doing ERISA work. My existing client base also exploded in other ways. This new work was super sophisticated, complicated, and again, not traditionally performed by my group.

made this a short stop. I was not going to stand in long lines on my last day in France. Instead, I went off for a serious Paris walkabout. I hit all the major sites, did some window shopping, bought some Euro pants and shoes. While exploring the sights, I was bombarded with emails that tested my peaceful state of mind. I remained peaceful and responded to each email in a detached manner and continued to enjoy a sweet afternoon in Paris. I was not going to make the "emergencies" *my* personal issues. Later that night I wondered, *were the emails different or was I?*

I spent my last evening having dinner at a fancy restaurant, took a midnight walk (unfortunately, I did not run into Hemingway, *Midnight in Paris* style) and stopped at a couple of fancy bars along the way. I even joined some locals for a smoke (cigarettes of course). At the last bar, it hit me, like a two-by-four to my forehead— my Adventure was over. I knew, without hesitation, taking an adult time-out was the right thing to do. I also felt totally complete (and I mean totally complete!). As I settled into bed that night, an overwhelming feeling of contentment came over me, and I felt as if I was returning to Big Law for the very first time.

Trust in Myself

My Gap Period provided a transformation within my soul. I discovered who I had become, but most importantly, who I wanted to be in my future. My foremost goal was to become conscious of the world that surrounds me. No more going with the flow, or being dissatisfied with middle management or hitting my head against the wall of life before going ten toes up. My adventurous soul had finally been (re)awakened.

Here I was on the cusp of my Gap Period ending, knowing that time sped by in a flash just as Nicole had predicted, and I was thankful I did not quit work but rather took a short adult time-out.

A REFLECTIVE MOMENT: It's not necessary to go to the extreme of quitting a job in order to take a break. A break, however, must be longer than a two-week vacation in Mexico sipping on a drink garnished with a colorful umbrella. You must be able to unplug completely to appreciate the career you created. Unplugging will force you to become selfish and live the way you are meant to live with a "with pleasure" attitude.

Leave With Quite a Story!

I was exhausted from the buildup of four-and-a-half months of living out of a backpack. I was looking forward to never seeing my clothes again (except my Zegna shoes). While flying over the Atlantic back to Newark, New Jersey, I could not help but think of my days on the container ship with Nicholas, Edmund, Nesto, and of course, my Ukrainian friends. My container ship voyage was such an excellent way to begin. Launching this Adventure with no TSA was truly delightful in comparison to the security mess at the Paris airport. Paris TSA took two carabiners that were attached to my backpack for my entire trip. France can be so French at times.

I was really looking forward to getting home, seeing my kids and my dogs. On the way to the Paris airport, I received an unexpected call from my youngest, and we had a great conversation. My oldest sent me an email welcoming me home, and my daughter sent me beautiful pictures of my smiling grandson. I was touched to know they were looking forward to dad being home. I feel good knowing I have done right by them, and I hope they will not forget my Adventure as their careers unfold. My legacy is that I was living life to the fullest (and they should too).

Newark: Culture Shock

I landed in the city from where it all began. The container ships were in plain view from the airport. As I made my way through security, I was in a complete culture shock watching people running to and from gates. It was overwhelming being in America again. The suits were everywhere. I walked to the United lounge, and all the travelers seemed stressed, overweight and pounding on some form of scotch/vodka/gin in an attempt to lighten an otherwise dull way of being while talking frantically on their Bluetooth earpieces. I was officially back in the States!

Own Your Tomorrow

I calmly waited for my connecting flight to Houston when I realized taking my adult time-out wasn't that big of a risk. Unlike the author in the book *Eat Pray Eat,* where he realized you didn't need to travel to India to find happiness (and the like), you do need to take an adult time-out to see where you are headed and what you need to do to make a course correction in your station in life. A simple two-week vacation in Mexico drinking Coronas on the beach or a long golfing weekend in Scottsdale are no substitutes if you want a life-altering adventure.

Clear Your Mind of "Can't"

No matter what my short-term or long-term career plans turn out to be, taking this Adventure was not a mistake. This Adventure was my number one career highlight (as of September 2013). I feel much more aware of who I am and where I want to go in this world. But most importantly, I was getting back to that Blue Eyed Man with an awakened adventurous soul (and sole ☺).

PART III

BEHIND BLUE EYES

CHAPTER FIFTEEN

BEHIND BLUE EYES

Back in early 2013, my goal was to rediscover the man behind my blue eyes. All I ever knew was what I had become—a successful lawyer. Deep down, however, I knew I was more than that. This "self-discovery" (oh, how I detest words like that) was not about the Firm or Big Law, it was about me. As my Adventure unfolded, I caught a glimpse of the man who had not let his light shine for a long time, and as my Adventure came to an end, this is what I unearthed:

1. I had become stuck and subconsciously accepted the frustrations of the ordinary—and I am not the type to be satisfied with just ordinary.

2. I created an image that did not reflect who I was and conformed to a life of what others expected of me. My daily routine consumed my life. I had become automatic, completely robotic and intensely focused on the almighty billable hour until I had lost who I was. I was treading water, and it sometimes felt as if I was drowning.

3. I am a risk taker. I do not do status quo very well. I don't want to be remembered for the numbers of hours billed. I want to be remembered as the partner who would stop at nothing to transform an ERISA practice.

4. I am an adventurous soul. My heart's one true desire is to explore the world. My old poor soul was buried, resembling an expired passport collecting dust in a dresser drawer.

5. I am a genuine wanderlust. Although my soles may be lost in a city in Africa, my soul is no longer lost. It is an exceptionally freeing way to live.

6. I have a curious soul, and this curiosity was a catalyst in making this Adventure happen. I am curious as to what life has to offer, of what is out there and what I can bring into my work through my experiences. Curiosity may have killed the cat, but it is what motivates me. I love the unknown of what life brings, the who knows and the what ifs. I love the rush of climbing a mountain, especially the areas where you cross over 1,000 feet of deep blue (and ever so beautiful) crevasses or moments when you need to kiss the side of a mountain to prevent falling to your death. Ironically, this makes me feel alive, and it is at those times where new ideas are born.

7. Most Big Law lawyers have mastered the art of small talk. I am not good with small talk or speaking about trivial matters. I enjoy discussing substantive matters, matters that have meaning to both the person I am speaking with as well as to myself. I enjoy ideas that others share with me and the energy that is derived when their soul is awakened. Especially since my soul has been awakened.

8. My Adventure was not about finding myself but remembering who I've been all along.

I hope that I will never be afraid to fail.

—Walt Disney

What Comes After the Letter "Z"?

Every wise man started out by asking many questions.

—Chinese Proverb

As my Gap Period concluded, I developed a curiosity of what would come next. I unplugged from being a billing machine and created serenity where my past sufferings previously lived. A fear of the unknown hadn't crawled into that empty space either. It was no longer a concern to me. I was free. It was in this state of pure freedom that I looked forward to a future of an adventurous life.

Looking back at my creation of this Adventure, I am heavenly pleased for taking it and truly feel that everyone should do the same at some point in their life. This experience made me realize who I really wanted to be going forward and what I needed to do in order to transform into that person.

I hope you have enjoyed my Adventure and that you take a page from my crazy playbook and experience life from a different perspective, and who knows, you may reach your "zone of genius."

Ciao,

Yours in travel,

Mark

The end of all our exploring will be to arrive where we started and know the place for the first time.

—T.S. Eliot, "Little Gidding"

EPILOGUE

In the weeks that followed my return to Big Law, I found myself thinking about the Kili priest's sermon on finding one's treasure. I found my treasure. It was very simple. It was to live the life I was meant to live and to allow my adventurous soul to awaken from years of dormancy. My treasure was certainly not located behind a desk nor accumulating in some Fidelity Investment account.

I lived in a completely different world during my Adventure. There were no time sheets and no dress codes to adhere to. I was completely aware of the world I was living in. I had a different appreciation of my career, and I felt renewed and alive once again. One may say there is something extraordinary about leaving a career and returning with a fresh spirit and realizing, and more importantly appreciating, how fabulous it really can be.

My first week back at Big Law seemed as if I walked into a live recording of a movie, a reality show of sorts, spoken in the third person but that third person was me. People approached me as if I was still that poor old soul who simply cranked out ERISA billable hours. Some were happy to see me and some were surprised I returned. Several were resentful and made unnecessary comments. I became fascinated with the range of reactions and found it interesting to hear their perspectives. One lawyer approached me and asked, "Did you lose all of your clients?" Another asked whether my pay was reduced. I also met with a retired partner who continues to come to work on a daily basis and was genuinely interested and intrigued to hear all about my Adventure. All remarkable sentiments on my first few days back. These conversations seemed to be talking about a person who left the Firm four months ago and not the man behind the blue eyes.

I was, overall, enjoying life and letting people know my Adventure was spectacular, enlightening and most of all, that I was doing great. After meeting with the Firm's benefits consultant, she mentioned that I had become a different person (she also wanted me to continue my blog), and she was right. I was a different person. Threatened lawsuits over pension contributions, forced retirements, etc. were no longer *my personal* issues. Stepping back from my high station in life did not drive me to a monastic lifestyle, but it made me commit to living a more conscious and experience-filled life. I was excited about *me* and being the person behind my blue eyes.

Since my return, my adventurous life continued. I explored Japan (Bill Murray style), Iceland (Walter Mitty style), made a return trip to South Africa, explored Victoria Falls, summited the tallest peak in Europe, as well as Mount Rainer, enjoyed a Christmas in Quebec City, searched for puffins and icebergs in Newfoundland and Orca whales in the San Juan Islands to list only a few of my most memorable post-Adventure explorations. All in all, life was good.

I received a note from a colleague during my first week back, and it said, "You are a wonderful free spirit—wish there were more like you." All I can say is I am satisfied becoming the man I was meant to be in this lifetime.

Thank you for reading my book.

Back to Work
Ciao

APPENDIX A

"ONLY IF EVERYONE KNEW WHAT I NOW KNOW"

One can spend all kinds of good money on therapists, self-help books, seminars and the like to have the illusion of finding out what is wrong, hard and unfair with Big Law as a pretext to quitting. The easier route is to take an adult time-out (ATO). I never knew an ATO would solve the "wrong," "hard" and "unfair" of work and lead to a transformative career full of satisfaction, curiosity and gratitude.

When I arrived back to the 47th floor, all I could think of was if every lawyer in Big Law knew what I now know, they would all be writing their very own Jerry McGuire manuscript and taking an ATO. But since my life had changed and I was putting me first, this is what I knew:

> 1. This Adventure had matured me. All adolescent anx-
> ieties about *Where will future projects come from? Will I
> have enough money to retire?* and *Will I have health insurance
> post-working years?* have disappeared.

2. Big Law allowed me to play at a level unparalleled to any other. It has allowed me, as a lawyer, to work on the big stage of my profession. But it was only after stepping out of Big Law and taking my ATO that I fully embraced its magnificence as a career.

3. By unplugging, I was able to connect with a part of myself that I knew existed but needed to be awakened. My Adventure saved me time, energy and anxiety…(aka stress) of having to quit my Firm and establish a law practice down the street.

4. The old school approach of work was to be retained by as many clients as possible and bill, bill and bill. In other words, make hay while the sun shines is the motto of Big Law. But I decontextualized this way of working into more work by focusing on fewer clients with more client attention (SA style), and profitable revenue was the result. This alternative service model benefited the clients, the Firm and, most of all, me.

5. One needs to take an ATO in order to make space for expansion. Rushing from one project to another has the effect of restricting the growth of a law practice. There is no time left in the day to expand a practice. By unplugging and taking my ATO, it created the space I needed in order to expand and transform my ERISA practice from simply drafting 401(k) plans to sophisticated and complex ERISA transactions. My ATO also created space for my NYC gig to unfold. It may not have transpired if I continued to keep my head down and crank out thousands of billable hours as previously expected on the 47th floor.

6. I redefined what it meant to be a trusted advisor.[7] Like most changes, this became a journey and a work in progress, but it was happening.

7. My Adventure allowed me to create *time*. I spend my time more wisely now. I work just as hard as I did pre-adult time-out, if not harder, but I also know when my work is done for the day. I no longer unwind by watching SportsCenter with a cold beer in hand. Instead, since my return, I completed two half Ironmans, a full Ironman and numerous marathons and half marathons (all the while keeping work going on all cylinders).

8. I have met some amazing new friends. It has been refreshing to meet people from different walks of life and different careers. The lesson here is that one should get out into the community, meet new people and experience a different slice of life. You never know where this will lead you—perhaps you may just meet your next client?

---

7 By taking on a smaller number of clients and allocating projects among other Firm lawyers, I effectively shifted client engagement from my shoulders. This then allowed me to focus more on how best to serve the client.

APPENDIX B

FOUR YEARS OUT

When I landed back in Houston in September 2013, a gnawing fear was that I would slowly, and sub-consciously, revert to my old way of being. That is, I would again become concerned with the almighty billable hour target.

But as I finish this book in the spring of 2017, four years later, I am thankful that I never regressed into an hourly billing machine. Who I previously was remained so far behind me that it was not even in my rearview mirror. Change had occurred. I had become a different lawyer with a transformed career, and I was extremely happy with my work-life balance. Colleagues have taken notice as to how much I enjoy being an ERISA lawyer and are no longer surprised by where my adventures lead.

The Adventure was about unbecoming everything that was not "me" so that I could truly become who I was meant to be. My life slowed and the roses smelled great. The curiosity of what would happen next also created an excitement in my daily existence. I continued to live an adventurous life with many travels to various off-the-beaten-path destinations.

With respect to my career on the 47th floor (and the 30th floor in

NYC), my client engagement and their satisfaction have been incredible. I scaled my client base and focused on approximately ten main clients, and together, the clients and I are both satisfied. Focusing on fewer clients has generated an increase in client satisfaction, and from a business standpoint, growth in Firm profits. There are times I am amazed that I pulled off an adult time-out, but in these rare moments, I remind myself that it was the best move I ever made. Every lawyer (or anyone in a demanding position) should consider taking an adult time-out and travel down a different path to see where their life is headed or whether their career is buried like an expired passport stuck in a dresser drawer. Don't let that be you.

Yours *still* in travel,

Mark

HIGHLIGHTS OF ADVENTURE 2013

My Adventure was nothing less than spectacular. Every highlight arose out of an unplanned day that transpired into an adventure in itself.

1. Traveling across the Atlantic Ocean on a container ship carrying 4,000 containers of presumably crap was the perfect way to begin my Gap Period. I had no idea what to expect, but it was definitely exceptional. Samuel Johnson and his writings were transformative. The routine of cocktail hour with Nicholas and jamming with Nesto on our guitars while sitting in the kitchen was just plain awesome and unforgettable.

2. Italy, Round 1. Showing up at an incredibly fancy hotel with smelly boots and trekking pants and being allowed to check-in. I believe I was allowed to check-in simply because I had a reservation (and a credit card that worked).

3. South Africa was humbly beautiful, a place that I could

see myself living. My African experience got off to a
fabulous start. From climbing Table Mountain to a tour
of the wine country to hanging with an interesting lot
in Port St. Johns, it was all a truly amazing experience.

4. Mozambique. Nothing beats crashing a wedding,
hanging with newlyweds and unexpectedly with the
US Ambassador at a blowout party that went on well
into the night.

5. Uganda. ALWAYS expect the unexpected. From
dinner with the CDC to drinks with a prostitute to
climbing an incredible mountain range and ending up
with a silverback and his family, Uganda is a destination
for all adventurous travelers.

6. Tanzania. It was all about stepping on the Roof of
Africa. I'm glad I made it up and down Kili and got in
the best shape ever. And yes, the Rwenzoris were much
more difficult than the Kili climb.

7. Italy, Round 2. Nothing beat staying in a trailer park
and listening to folk music at a tarantella festival.

8. France. I tricked my mind into thinking I could run
a marathon.

9. Writing the blog. The only thing more fun than writing
a daily post was reading feedback from friends, specifically knowing my blog had become pillow talk.

10. My flight home. I had never felt more complete in
life. This Adventure made me jazzed about going back
to my career as never before. I never felt this energized
after a one week vacation.

APPENDIX D

INSPIRATIONAL QUOTES

"Whether I shall turn out to be the hero of my own life, or whether that station will be held by anybody else, these pages must show."
—Charles Dickens, *David Copperfield*

"Faith is taking the first step even when you don't see the whole staircase."
—Martin Luther King, Jr.

"A lot of us first aspired to far-ranging travel and exotic adventure early in our teens…Thus, when we allow ourselves to imagine as we once did, we know, with a sudden jarring clarity, that if we don't go right now, we're never going to do it. And we'll be haunted by our unrealized dreams…"
—Tim Cahill

"People who travel the world aren't running away from life. Just the opposite. Those that break the mold, explore the world, and live on their own terms are running toward true living, in my opinion. We have a degree of freedom a lot of people will never experience. We get to be the captains of our ships. But it is a freedom we chose to have. We looked around and said, 'I want something different.' It was that freedom and attitude I saw in travelers years ago that inspired me to do what

I am doing now. I saw them break the mold and I thought to myself, 'Why not me too?' I'm not running away. I am running towards the world and my idea of life. "
—Nomadic Matt, Blogger

"The tragedy of life doesn't lie in not reaching your goal. The tragedy lies in having no goal to reach. "
—Benjamin E. Mays

"All courses of action are risky, so prudence is not in avoiding danger, but calculating risk and acting decisively. Make mistakes of ambition and not mistakes of sloth. Develop the strength to do bold things, not the strength to suffer. "
—Niccolò Machiavelli, *The Prince*

"Life can only be understood backwards; but it must be lived forwards. "
—Søren Kierkegaard

"Most of us abandoned the idea of a life full of adventure and travel sometime between puberty and our first job. Our dreams died under the dark weight of responsibility. Occasionally the old urge surfaces, and we label it with names that suggest psychological aberrations: the big chill, a midlife crisis. "
—Tim Cahill

"Only those who will risk going too far can possibly find out how far one can go. "
—T.S. Eliot, Preface to Harry Crosby's *Transit of Venus*

"Only put off until tomorrow what you are willing to die having left undone. "
—Pablo Picasso

"Fear isn't only a guide to keep us safe; it's also a manipulative emotion that can trick us into living a boring life…the great stories go to those who don't give in to fear. "
—Donald Miller, *A Million Miles in a Thousand Years: What I Learned While Editing My Life*

"He went to Paris looking for answers to questions that bothered him so…

married an actress…they had a good life…20 years slipped away…hopped on a freighter, skidded the ocean and left…without a sound."
                                        —Jimmy Buffet, "He Went to Paris"

"Peace be with you…And with your spirit…And protect me from all anxiety as I go…"
                                        —Rite of Peace at a Roman Catholic Mass

"We are all brothers and sisters."
—Captain Alex from the CMA CGM Jamaica (Describing the relationship between the people of the Ukraine and Russia)

"The necessity of setting the world at a distance from us, when we are to take a survey of ourselves, has sent many from high stations to the severities of a monastic life."
                                        —Samuel Johnson, *The Rambler* No. 23

"If we are going to do anything significant with life, we sometimes have to move away from it—beyond the usual measurements. We must occasionally follow visions and dreams."
                                        —Fr. Bede Jarrett

"You won't kill yourself by doing it; you will kill yourself by not doing it."
                                        —Unknown

"You can check-out anytime you like, but you can never leave."
                                        —The Eagles, "Hotel California"

"Disguising our insignificance by the dignity of hurry."
                                        —Samuel Johnson, *The Rambler* No. 142

"So at the very least, ask yourself this hypothetical question today, 'if I had no fear, if I imagine that failure is not an option, what would I do and when would I do it?' The answer, I suspect, would be 'now.'"
                                        —Alastair Humphreys, Blogger

"I am sitting at the railway station with a ticket for my destination…"
—Simon & Garfunkel, "Homeward Bound"

"It is easier to stay out than to get out."
—Mark Twain

"And then there is the most dangerous risk of all—the risk of spending your life not doing what you want on the bet you can buy yourself the freedom to do it later."
—Randy Komisar, *The Monk and the Riddle: The Education of a Silicon Valley Entrepreneur*

"Insanity: doing the same thing over and over again and expecting different results."
—Albert Einstein, (attributed)

"Better weight than wisdom a traveler cannot carry."
—Viking Proverb

"Nobody ever died of discomfort, yet living in the name of comfort has killed more ideas, more opportunities, more actions, and more growth than everything else combined. Comfort Kills!"
—T. Harv Eker

"Most of us have two lives. The life we live, and the unlived life within us. Between the two stands Resistance."
—Steven Pressfield, *The War of Art*

"The world is a book and those who do not travel read only one page."
—St. Augustine of Hippo

"Great things are done when men and mountains meet."
—William Blake

"They succeed because they think they can."

—Virgil

"Be more like the man that you were made to be . . ."
—Mumford & Sons, "Sigh No More"

"Because in the end, you won't remember the time you spent working in the office or mowing your lawn. Climb that goddamn mountain."
—Jack Kerouac, *The Dharma Bums*

"There are two primary choices in life: to accept conditions as they exist, or accept the responsibility for changing them."
—Denis Waitley

"Be kind, for everyone you meet is fighting a battle you know nothing about."
—Wendy Mass, *The Candymakers*

"Please make sure that you secure your oxygen mask before helping others."
—United Airlines

"I hope that I will never be afraid to fail."
—Walt Disney

"Every wise man started out by asking many questions."
—Chinese Proverb

"The end of all our exploring will be to arrive where we started and know the place for the first time."
—T.S. Eliot, "Little Gidding"

ABOUT THE AUTHOR

Mark is a successful ERISA lawyer at one of the most prestigious international law firms. He has developed a sophisticated and complex ERISA practice and is recognized as one of the top ERISA lawyers. However, Mark's adventurous side was clouded by the heavy demands of law, and in the middle of his rising career, and with a huge leap of faith, he asked for and received an unprecedented adult time-out. His time-out began on a container ship crossing the Atlantic with 16 crew members and four Ukrainian officers, all of whom spoke little English, and then headed towards the back roads of Africa, Italy and France.

What Mark did not expect to discover on his journey was the

reawakening of his spirit. It was the beginning of a new life feeding his soul with experiences outside the walls of an office on the 47th floor. This was the rebirth of Mark S. Miller.

What transpired afterward is what matters most.

Mark took what he learned from his experiences on this trip and applied them to his practice. Mark's revenue increased with a surge of new business traditionally not performed, without increasing his billing hours. He firmly believes that lawyers will undeniably transform their careers by stepping out of their routine of billing hours with a break that is longer than a two-week vacation sipping Coronas on a beach. He believes the road less traveled (aka taking an adult time-out) is best. Temporarily unplugging from a demanding career, rather than quitting, will allow you to rediscover how marvelous your career really can be.

Warning: taking this type of break may send one from the high station of Big Law to the severities of a monastic life.

Visit Mark at

myadulttimeout.com

for more on how to incorporate travel into your career!

DEDICATED TO:

_____

BIG LAW LAWYERS WHO HAVE YET
TO LIVE LIFE TO THE FULLEST

YOUR LIFE IS STILL OUT THERE

CPSIA information can be obtained
at www.ICGtesting.com
Printed in the USA
LVOW12s2326200318

570605LV00001B/182/P